The
GREAT
RESET

INDIA · SINGAPORE · MALAYSIA

Notion Press

No.8, 3rd Cross Street,
CIT Colony, Mylapore,
Chennai, Tamil Nadu – 600004

First Published by Notion Press 2020
Copyright © Yadunath S 2020
All Rights Reserved.

ISBN 978-1-64919-573-9

The
GREAT
RESET

The Unfolding Bear Market and
the Opportunity of a Lifetime

YADUNATH S

INDIA · SINGAPORE · MALAYSIA

INDICACADEMY

INDIC PLEDGE

- *I celebrate our civilisational identity, continuity & legacy in thought, word and deed.*

- *I believe our indigenous thought has solutions for the global challenges of health, happiness, peace and sustainability.*

- *I shall seek to preserve, protect and promote this heritage and in doing so,*
  - *discover, nurture and harness my potential,*
  - *connect, cooperate and collaborate with fellow seekers,*
  - *advance diversity and inclusivity in the society.*

ABOUT INDIC ACADEMY

Indic Academy is a non-traditional 'university' for traditional knowledge. We seek to bring about a global renaissance based on Indic civilizational and indigenous thought. We are pursuing a multidimensional strategy across time, space and cause by establishing centers of excellence, transforming intellectuals and building an ecosystem.

Indic Academy is pleased to support this book.

DISCLAIMER

All observations, facts and comments mentioned in this work with reference to markets, in general and with specific reference to a stock, index and other instruments are intended to create an awareness and deepen knowledge among the investing and trading community.

Nothing stated in this book is to be construed directly or indirectly as an invitation or solicitation to buy/sell/trade any stock, index, derivative and other instruments.

The author or the publisher do not purport to make any recommendations to buy or sell stock, other instruments and derivatives.

The author sincerely urges the reader to always adopt proper risk management norms and actively manage one's risks when dealing with stocks and other market instruments.

Dedicated to

my late parents, who ingrained in me the quest to pursue knowledge and truth

my loving wife, Savitha, who has stood by me through the ups and downs and

my lovely daughters, Srushti and Krittika, who have given meaning and purpose to our lives

"Faith is the bird that feels the light and sings when the dawn is still dark. The people who change our lives the most begin to sing to us while we are still in darkness. If we listen to their song, we will see the dawning of a new part of ourselves."

– **Rabindranath Tagore**

CONTENTS

PART II – A BUBBLE READY TO BUST

PART III – LOOKING BEYOND THE HORIZON

PREFACE

Men wish to uncover what lies beyond the horizon in the unknown future but often do not recognize what is hiding in plain sight. As the new year 2020 started, the headline in a leading daily screamed that emerging markets will likely have a happy new year quoting the head of a leading research firm who had said that structurally we were close to the next bull market. So much for a research firm that is employing well paid analysts and supposedly sifting through decades of stock data and mulling over tonnes of economic, company and industry data. Little did the guy imagine that we had knowingly or unknowingly wandered into the edge of a cliff not knowing there was a deep abyss below.

The stock markets across the world crashed an unprecedented 40% (BSE SENSEX by 39.3% to be precise) in a span of two months and a major chunk of that occurred in less than a month's time. It was suddenly like the ground under your feet started shifting and falling apart. Oil prices hit zero and briefly even hit negative territory, something unprecedented. Several investors saw their wealth disappear right in front of their own eyes. It didn't seem to matter whether you were directly exposed to equities or mutual funds. The consequent rush to sell mutual funds brought such pressure on redemption, draining liquidity in the debt market and nearly resulting in a tremor. In fact, one major mutual fund decided to shut down several debt fund schemes abruptly, something that had never happened before.

It was like a big fat thumb from the heavens just pressed the factory reset button.

We live in a seemingly sophisticated world -- or at least we like to think so - surrounded by gadgets, computers and other devices of sorts. We are working hard to predict a Tsunami minutes or hours in advance to save human lives. We are building mathematical models that will help predict earthquakes and so on. Of course, nothing matters more in the world than saving precious human lives and everything else comes next. Yet, a financial tsunami, most severe in our lifetimes, hit us suddenly and wiped out investors and retirees' wealth within a span of six to eight weeks as if someone forcibly wiped the contents of a whiteboard before you took down notes.

Was it all sudden really, as most of us may like to say? Did it really strike us without an advance warning? I am not talking about making predictions here. Predictions are hard to come by and even when made, most people don't take them seriously. We have heard those predicting end of the world and here we are as a human race intact and learning to survive the most infectious pandemic yet. My question is more humble and perhaps more practical. An advance warning would have helped anticipate, prepare and act much better.

The NIFTY was ballooning (and BSE SENSEX too) and there was unabated optimism and exuberance in the build-up to the crash. During this period, there were clear indications that the bull run was running out of fuel and cracks were developing. I would be covering those in detail with illustrations within the pages of this book.

In the months preceding the crash, I had written to one of the leading capital market magazines as well as a leading financial daily to warn about an impending correction and had explained with price charts along with my analysis. I was somehow hopeful of getting my views published in advance, but it was hard and nearly impossible to get the attention of media.

In Dec'19, I had met one of the largest fund managers in Mumbai, and had hinted about a possible market correction according to the models and future price projections, which I was working on. Not surprisingly, the response I heard was that there is no major reason why the markets will correct now or in the near future. *That's exactly the nature of bubbles, people just don't see them.* The irony is that when markets are at the top, the sentiment is at its peak and nearly everyone seems to unanimously think that the good times will last forever. The newspaper headline I pointed at the outset above is a solid example.

Bubbles and busts keep alternating as history shows time and again. Unless you were a millennial or a post millennial, most of you would distinctly remember the dot com bubble that shook the world in the year 2000 followed again by the financial crisis in the year 2008 that shook the markets like never before. Major bull runs are invariably followed by countertrend moves in the opposite direction. The bubble peaks - like 2000 and 2008 - are invariably accompanied by steep corrections and both the phases are inseparable and inevitable, if we care to look at history. The fact that markets undergo correction, now and then, is natural and considered healthy. The most recent bull run culminating in the crash that started in Feb'20 - also the longest bull run ever in history - went on far too long and the resulting fall was naturally severe too. Ironically, someone once said that the only thing that history showed is that we humans don't learn from history.

Interestingly about a couple years ago, I came across the Harvard economist Harry Dent, who had been screaming that markets have been on steroids and the financial asset prices, including real estate, had become unsustainable. Harry attributed this mostly to the unprecedented and continued injection of liquidity into the system ever since the financial crisis in 2008 unfolded. The proponents of the 90-year market cycle (Andy Pancholi, in particular) had been screaming loud since mid-2018 about a financial tsunami and a repeat of the Great Depression of 1929-32.

No one could have foreseen the occurrence of the pandemic and its precise impact on the market, but a major price correction and market slowdown was overdue and inevitable.

The purpose of writing this book is to share intelligence based on observed facts that can be inferred by anyone who has an open mind. You will gain a perspective to look at the markets much to your advantage and walk with your eyes and ears open. Should you happen to be a seasoned investor, it will remind you of the things that possibly escaped your notice and if you already noticed as may be the case, sharing similar thoughts is reinforcing and causes a higher reverberation.

This book has been divided into three logical portions. Part II deals with the precursors to a late-stage and an exuberant bull market, alerting that the market had topped and the bubble would eventually explode. Part I deals with some preparatory topics before delving into Part II. Part III is looking ahead and futuristic.

It's best to read in the order in which the chapters are arranged. If you are short on time and patience and wish to get ahead, you could choose to skip Part I and start with Part II right away. Please do note that Chapter 4 in Part I will help better appreciate the contents in Chapter 8 in Part II.

It is too early to say and though I don't wish to get ahead of myself, it would be my endeavour to write a sequel to this book expanding the outlook in Part III when the time is ripe and we reached the right juncture.

I have heard that some of the greatest wealth ever built in the United States in the twentieth century was after the Great Depression and the accompanying crash in the years 1929 through 1932. I sincerely wish that this book opens your eyes to the best investment opportunity in a lifetime and to build wealth for a lifetime and possibly for generations to come. We are at the cusp of the next bull wave that will likely kickstart towards 1921-22.

The economic growth and rise in the financial markets in the last two decades is only the tip of the iceberg and a primer to what potential may be expected in the decades to come.

As more and more ordinary people invest and grow their wealth, the society becomes prosperous and people yearn to achieve higher material and spiritual goals. As more people start aspiring higher and higher and share their wealth with the less privileged, so the world becomes a better place in our own living time.

PART I
THE TOOLBOX

CHAPTER ONE

THE WORLD IS ONE EXTENDED GLOBAL MARKET

They say that when the US catches cold, the world sneezes. Stocks, Currencies, Gold and Oil are all globally traded. Derivatives and exotic instruments are traded in millions everyday more than you can imagine.

There is no national border for trading. The index of nearly all major countries is available in one form or the other across geographical borders. The world is one marketplace. India's very own NIFTY 50 is traded in trading platforms across the world using some proxy or other.

THE WORLD IS ONE EXTENDED MARKET....

Introduction

In the years 1929-1932, North America was hit by what has since been referred as the Great Depression. Certain cycles experts had pointed out that there is a 90-year cycle that goes on and that put a big question mark on the 90-th anniversary that fell in 2019. Truth be told most markets had peaked in 2019 or at the beginning of 2020, though the drastic slide occurred only a few months later in Mar' 20.

Well, India didn't have a stock market history that went far back in time but that doesn't prevent us from drawing inference from other countries' history and experience and more so in an integrated world where economic growth or slackening has a cascading effect. We are in no way insulated or ring fenced in any manner, so to speak. In other words, when it comes to market trending over the longer term, it would be wiser to look at the financial markets history of the United States and extrapolate it because what hit the NYSE and NASDAQ does invariably hit the LSE, TSE and BSE of the world. Well, do they indeed affect other markets? The experience has been that it does so and let's look at it below.

Certain academicians would like us to believe that markets move randomly and can't be explained. Their observation is only superficially true to the extent that there is an element of randomness in markets, when observed too closely at shorter time intervals. But, it would be inaccurate to say that such randomness constitutes an entirety and it would do a disservice to all the evidence that goes to show otherwise. There is abundant scientifically proven materials that go to show that markets often follow patterns and such patterns repeat themselves over time and again. The specific patterns are often followed by a certain kind of predictable price behaviour that do provide advance alert quite so often about the imminent market moves and the broad direction in store.

When observed over the longer term, markets appear to move in cycles. While stocks and currency pairs may behave in a certain way due to local factors specific to the country, there's a certain commonality in underlying trend, broadly speaking.

It is important to understand what moves the markets. Many experienced traders believe that smart money moves the markets. Smart money essentially means institutional money brought in by large investors including insurance firms, pension funds, hedge funds and mutual funds aside from certain high net worth investors dealing in large volumes. The smart money moves the markets.

Markets are not ruled or even controlled by a select few players. Mr.Market is bigger than everyone and no player gets bigger than the market regardless of how resourceful an institution or person may be.

The 2008 crisis

The entire financial world was rocked in 2008 due to a liquidity crisis and the mortgage crisis exploded in the United States. The trigger then was provided by the Lehman Brothers (then a much respected and world renowned US investment firm) folding up overnight. Left to themselves, AIG, one of the largest insurers in the world and Citibank, among the best known international banks would have ceased to exist and they were on the deathbed. The US government salvaged AIG for it didn't wish for a crisis of faith to erupt in the insurance industry, which would have set a bad precedent forever to come. Citibank was salvaged eventually too.

During the 2008 financial crisis, the US stock markers and of course, the Dow Jones and S & P 500 took a big hit. But you'll be surprised to note that nearly all major stock indices in the world including FTSE 100 (London), DAX (Frankfurt), NIKKEI 225 in Tokyo and a host of other indices across France, Spain, Luxembourg and elsewhere in the world took a big hit too. India's own NIFTY, BSE SENSEX and BANK NIFTY took a big hit in 2008 and that remains a major bottom till date until the most recent crash in 2020, which incidentally is the subject matter of this book.

Connected Markets

We are not about to deep dive into why the markets are inter-connected across the world and I don't claim to be the best person to answer that question. That said, I do wish to touch on the contours to some extent.

Well, each country is different, industrialized to varying extent, has its own economic policies and rate of growth, so I am not for a moment suggesting that everyone grows or decays at the same rate, which is economically not true and doesn't make any sense either. Developed countries like Germany and Australia export big time to China. Germany exports its sophisticated machinery and automobiles to China while Australia exports minerals. If Chinese economy were to shrink, it reduces consumption and constricts exports from Germany to China and thus impacting their fortunes. So, the fortunes of one big economy is not entirely independent of rest of the world and it impacts cascadingly other economies around the world.

Central Banks in the developed world, especially in the United States and other parts of the developed world had created unprecedented liquidity in the years following the 2008 Financial Crisis to keep their respective economies from sinking down. The direct intervention by Governments and Central Banks in the markets had become more pronounced in the last decade or so compared to earlier. This did universal damage since the combination of abundant liquidity and lower interest rate yields in debt market eventually impacted equity markets driving up stock prices. The markets moved up insanely in the years following because of the extra money being pumped in billions had to go somewhere and inflating financial assets beyond a reasonable point and we ended up with the longest bull run in history. This inevitably led to inflated asset prices across the sectors, be it real estate, Gold or stocks. Especially, in the two to three years preceding market crash, markets went way too high into a bubble zone without any attending rationality and it was only a matter of time that the bubble popped up.

Another important dimension is that the major pension funds, hedge funds and mutual funds of humongous sizes invest across the borders - directly or indirectly through derivatives - and that is potentially a major contributor for the common impact on markets beyond the borders. Truth be told, the reason NIFTY went on spiraling forward through 2019 despite slackness in the Indian economy was simply that overseas funds were continuing to pump in money in Indian stock markets (aside from mutual funds) and chasing select stocks. We will revisit this point in a later chapter.

A bubble in the United States effectively was problem enough for other markets across the world. You should understand early on this journey that we live in an increasingly integrated world and it is more true now than it has ever been before.

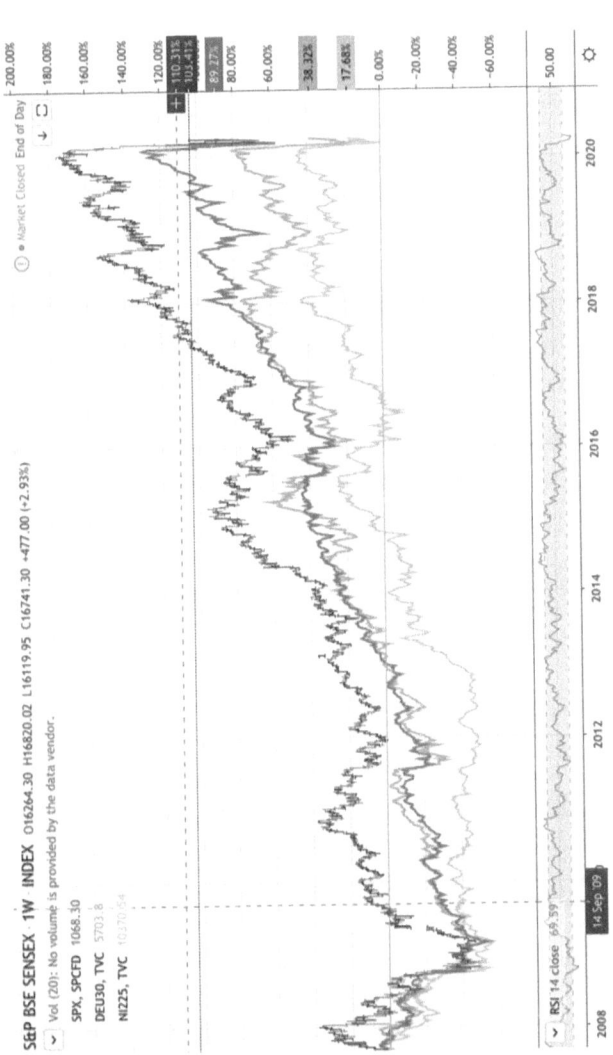

Figure: 1.1: Long term chart of key indices
Courtesy: Trading view

Look at the chart Figure 1.1. It is a weekly chart of key stocks indices across the world including USA, Germany, Japan and India. I could have added more but I liked to drive home my point without the chart getting way too cluttered to make any sense out of it.

The above chart is a weekly chart, meaning each single bar in the chart shows price movement for an entire week. The reason I picked a weekly chart as opposed to a daily or an hourly chart is that it shows the price trend of major stock indexes over a period of several years. The chart essentially covers the period since 2008, exactly when markets had hit a major bottom after the great financial crisis. In effect the above price chart spans the last major bottom and shows all the way until the present peak up until the Mar'20 crash just before writing this book.

Now, let us get to our point having set the context for the chart. Just look at the spikes and troughs. One can't help noticing how the ups and downs resemble remarkably closely across the different indices and surprisingly most of those look closely similar? A picture speaks a thousand words and more so at least in this picture . To me, this chart speaks volumes. There an uncanny alignment between the stock averages and indices across the world.

The ups and downs are closely similar not due to co-incidence or some random behavior. There is some universal frame in which world stock markets seem to move. Now, if I were to repeat that the world markets are interrelated, it shouldn't sound as alien as that sounded earlier.

The impact of heavy liquidation by Foreign Institutional Investors

I was talking to some industry experts in the Wealth Management industry *before* the crash and ironically enough I was asking them what will happen to Indian markets if the 'FII-s' start pulling the rug from under our feet. FIIs represent all the overseas dollars from the wealthiest institutions and hedge funds finding its way into Indian markets. I was told that such a scenario was unlikely to occur, since Mutual Funds have grown bigger and come to play a very significant role over the years.

The drastic fall in the financial markets during Mar'20 crash proved that fears were indeed correct and not unfounded. Markets started falling like a pack of cards when FII started selling stocks.

The stock markets crashed like never before between Feb and Mar'20. Many in the market were caught holding long positions and were caught panicking as markets started sliding like it has never happened in our lifetime before.

Once markets started falling, there was no stopping as institutions and retail traders alike started liquidating their positions. Those holding long positions through Futures had margin calls and had to cover their portfolio losses. There is little time and incentive to rationalize when panic reigns and unfortunately, panic triggers a herd behavior as traders start unloading their positions accelerating a downward spiral.

Once retail investors start selling shares and mutual fund units in hordes as happened recently, selling pressure increases due to mutual funds liquidating the positions since they have to settle the money to investors. Mutual Funds didn't cause the slide in the first place but they indirectly started participating and accelerating the fall once the price started falling.

The Foreign Institutional Investors were not presumably so much concerned about what was happening specific to Indian economy. It was driven by their own anticipation of a global slow down in the interconnected world. There were several other factors too that precipitated the fall.

Given the lock-down, Gold mining, production and transportation had nearly shut down and caused an unprecedented logistics crisis in moving physical gold (assuming anybody had adequate supply of physical gold in the first place). Thanks to the scarcity of physical Gold, bullion markets had become highly volatile with Gold prices swinging heavily. Highly leveraged Futures traders with huge positions had to cover their positions and this triggered large scale liquidation of other parts of their portfolio thereby creating a spiral.

CHAPTER TWO

CYLES, CYCLES & CYCLES

The laws of universe govern everything around us...the unseen hand is all pervading like gravity regardless of whether we are aware

CYCLES, CYCLES & CYCLES

There are cycles around us everywhere closely intertwined with our lives and often governing our lives one way or the other. There are solar cycles, lunar cycles, economic cycles and revolutionary cycles around us. Our lives are governed by cycles whether or not we recognise them and whether or not we remain ignorant.

The Great Wheel of time

The day and night form a cycle. One day is a cycle, because that's the time it takes for earth to rotate around itself. It takes about four minutes for our Mother Earth to move by about one degree and our Earth moves about 15 degrees by the hour. That should explain how we came to have 24 hours in a day. The ancient Indians used Ghatika as a measure of time and that meant 24 minutes. An entire day from one sunrise to the next sunrise consisted of 60 Ghatikas. We have only flipped it around and made 24 hours of 60 minutes each.

The Sun moves one zodiac sign at a time in about thirty days, which gives rise to a month. So, remember that when it's your birthday, the Sun is almost at the same point in the zodiac as on that day when you were born. (It's earth that is moving around the Sun, but as we live on earth, as viewed from earth it is only natural that it appears as if the Sun is moving around us. .

The moon takes about 27 days to complete one revolution around our Mother Earth and that relates to the menstrual cycle in women. The Sun is related to masculine and Moon is related to the feminine. The Sun is said to be the source of life. Moon derives its light source from the Sun and there will be only life on earth only as long as there is Moon.

How many of us are even aware that our breath actually shifts its path just about every couple hours from right to left and from left to right and so on and so forth. At any point in time, our breath is predominantly flowing through either nostril and not through both. That means, at a given point in time, one hemisphere in our brains is more active than the other. The purpose of meditating is to make the breath flow evenly through the channels, but delving into it is outside the scope of this book.

Our lives are more governed by the earth we live and the solar system that we live in than we presently understand and willing to acknowledge. Whether we choose to live a life of awareness and how consciously we go about from moment to moment in our lives is up to us to determine.

Most people out there in stocks trade for the short to medium term and a vast majority of them look out to make quick profits. At such short time intervals, cycles are hard to observe and track down. Watching minute by minute price ticks may give a kick or a sense of being busy but it's not a great way to trade as opposed to swing trading and trend trading.

The fact is that cycles occur at both short time intervals and long, but the short ones are too many and it's easy to get distracted. When one is too concerned with the short term, he or she is bound to miss the forest for trees. It's relatively easier to observe the impact of cycles in the long run and thankfully that is what has a potentially larger impact on everything we do.

I have reproduced below certain key cycles as heard from Andrew Pachholi, one of the cycle experts that I have come across. Andy appears to have compiled every minor and major movement that took place through centuries and starts to see an irrefutable pattern that is hard not to acknowledge. Andy runs a market timing report, a monthly publication that brings out key dates for indices and commodities on the basis of long term weekly and daily cycles for benefit of traders.

The Hong Kong pro-democracy protests lasted several months and hogged most part of 2019. There were times when it seemed to take an ugly turn but it brought Hong Kong economy to a grinding halt until the virus took that dubious role forward.

In *1959*, the well known Tibet rebellion took place against China and it was then that the Dalai Lama took refuge in India and he holds Indian citizenship till date. *Thirty years later in 1989*, there was a major pro-democracy revolution in Beijing when thousands of University students gathered in Beijing for days together and refused to vacate the Tiananmen Square.

On a certain day in May'89, it apparently turned very violent and went out of control that resulted in a massacre of unarmed students by Chinese military, unthinkable today.

Still thirty years later in 2019 - which is more recent and most of us should not have trouble recollecting - there were several months of pro-democracy rebellion in Hong Kong against the iron grip of Chinese government. *Is it a coincidence that these events occurred at thirty years intervals?*

There appears to be an approximate 18 year cycle, so to speak, that brings an occurrence of major health hazards. In the 1980-s AIDS/ HIV made major inroads and gradually by 1985, every region in the world had reported its occurrence making it a rampant global issue. In the year 2002, SARS first occurred in China and had claimed over 8000 lives in 26 countries by 2003. Years later in 2019, we are witnessing the ravaging Coronavirus unleashing its wrath on humanity.

The 1929 Great Depression

No one who is possibly alive today has seen the Great Depression in 1929. I came to know some years ago about the Great Depression that hit the United States in 1929 and was gripped by it until 1932. Well, at that point in time, the major stock indices like Dow Jones index were much smaller in absolute value as compared to present times. In percentage terms, the stocks took a significant hit and the effects of the Great Depression left an impact on an entire generation and its effect was felt for many years to come. In the second half of 1929, the Dow Jones industrial average fell rapidly by 50% within a span of a few months. Post a recovery until the second quarter of 1930, the Dow then fell gradually over the next two years until mid-1932 by as much as 90% of the peak value in 1929. In percentage terms, Dow has not dropped as significantly ever since until very recently. Compared to the first round drop of 50% in 1929, Dow fell by 38% in just a few weeks preceding Mar'20. Given the absolute value of Dow in 2020 as compared to a very nominal value of the index in 1929, the recent fall was indeed very scary and a roller coaster ride.

The question that rises next is that whether the Mar crash is a one-off drop does it indicate the onset of a major correction yet to come. There are reasons to believe that the correction is not over yet given the economic impact of virus-induced lock-down and its cascading effects on the economy, which is yet to come. Only time will reveal the final answer.

On the positive side, it is also a fact that some of the greatest wealth ever built by those who were wise enough to spot the opportunities post 1932 that nearly everyone else missed out due to the battering received in preceding years that invariably breeds alongside such steep corrections. and the pessimism, which had built and nearly everyone else was looking the other way.

Great wealth is built in the long run through long term investing. Whether one is being a trader who thrives on swings and trends or whether one is interested in building wealth in the long run, cycles matter and understanding them will help you get better in putting money to best use.

The wheel of time reigns over everything. There is a 30-year major cycle and a 45-year major cycle that have been well established. Both the 30-year cycles and 45-year cycles converge to render a 90-year cycle of vital significance.

Bubbles and Busts

The great Harvard economist, Harry Dent, is the go-to guy for all things to do with booms and busts and he lives and breathes cycles for a living. His extraordinary grasp of economic cycles and demographic patterns had uniquely equipped him in predicting bubbles, time and again. The guy has done extensive analysis that has helped him isolate and identify certain long term cycles, which clearly cause highs and lows and help predict bubbles.

Harry had predicted way ahead that the abundance of easy money had irreparably damaged the US economy and had inflated asset prices to unreasonable extent leading to a bubble in literally every asset category, be it real estate or financial assets like stocks. The financial markets were on a steroid thanks to availability of easy money and companies were buying back their own shares and the resulting higher EPS drove share prices even up without necessarily higher earnings and without expanding manufacturing capacities. Harry Dent and Andy Pancholi had both warned well ahead that a calamity was waiting and in my opinion, they were only off the mark in that they expected the crash to occur in 2019, but it turned out to be an all-time high for stocks. They were still too close in their prediction in that the decline started with the commencement of 2020 and I suppose you can't get more accurate than that in predicting longer term cycles spanning decades.

It was no longer an issue that concerned only Western countries. We live in an integrated world and this money found its way in millions being pumped into Indian stock markets. In the three years preceding the market crash, Indian economy was not doing anything great but the NIFTY stocks kept going higher and higher simply because of smart money chasing select stocks.

History has proved time and again only one thing. Cycles work because they are meant to. We only know that cycles exist, they inevitably occur like clock-work from time to time. It's entirely another debate as to why they occur and what may be giving rise to cycles.

It is plausible that since human behaviour like fear and greed remain the same and we are known to act in herds, there are common behavioural traits at times of boom and stress in our inhabited world. As long as basic human behaviour exists, these patterns seem to work. I envisage there is more to it than meets the eye and it is closely linked to planetary and astro cycles, but that's another discussion outside the scope of this book.

And every bubble has to break one time, it can be delayed and manipulated by governments and central banks but no one has the power to stop them eventually from bursting. In its latest avatar, the virus was beyond humans control and no central bank or government could do anything to stop it. If anything, the bubble swells only worse through such attempts and when they go bust later, its impact is even more severe than if it was allowed to go bust sooner.

Elliott Wave Models

Several decades ago, a man named R N Elliott came up with a brilliant proposition after closely studying Dow Jones index data over several years. Elliott must have been an unrelenting genius of sorts. Elliott theorized that prices move in so-called wave patterns and that such wave patterns are continuous and occur in fractals across all timeframes regardless of whether one observed price movements in minutes, hours, days or weeks. It's not possible to deal with Elliott wave rules and guidelines in this book but it is good to be aware of it. According to the wave model, the main trend always consisted of five waves while a corrective trend occurred in three waves in the opposite direction of the trend. This was a phenomenal observation and often helped analysts to understand whether a prevailing trend is the major impulse trend or a corrective trend.

He attributed the wave model to basic human behavior namely, fear and greed. The waves are more clearly pronounced in markets where there is high liquidity because those markets are involving more human emotions of fear and greed.

As long as basic human behavior governing markets remain, the stock market action which represents collective herd behavior driven by human emotions follows certain repeatable patterns. As economic growth occurs, optimism increases and gives rise to a healthy outlook. As this expands and grows higher and higher more and more people join the club adding to the exuberance.

Past experience has shown that optimism reins higher at market peaks just before the bubble explodes. In other words, very high levels of optimism and exuberance that nothing will ever go wrong is not a bullish sign but a bearish sign. Vice-versa, observed data in hindsight has proven that sober mood and skepticism reign high at market bottoms. In other words, extremely bearish outlook and sentiments are in fact signs of a bull market that is about to start. It may seem contradictory but expert Elliott practitioners use the sentiments to their advantage when trading.

We will see more of Elliott wave thinking and some illustrations in a later chapter.

CHAPTER THREE

THE BUBBLE OF A LIFETIME

The stocks were more overvalued now than they were anytime in 2000 and 2008…whoever didn't see it did not see the writing on the wall….or were just blindsided….

A BUBBLE BUILT UP OVER THE YEARS....

Most people I talked to would like to believe that we are not (were not, rather) in a bubble. I wonder, at times whether that's because of our inherent nature to want to stay optimistic and downplay information not fitting within our thought process. In my humble opinion, it's one thing to stay positive and entirely another thing to hypnotically believe that nothing can ever go wrong, which amounts to self-deception.

The Zero Hour

As I introduced in the previous chapter, when it comes to all things bubbles, the Harvard educated economist Harry Dent is one of the few experts. Harry is not necessarily a stock market expert, but he is a Harvard educated economist, who keeps a tight pulse on financial markets and possibly having studied the nature of bubbles more than anyone else. His track record speaks enough for him. The guy had amazingly predicted that Japanese economy would irreversibly slide down when it was at its peak in 1980 when everyone was betting that Japan would soon overtake the United States as the number one economy. He had also predicted the dotcom bubble in the year 2000 as well as the financial crisis in the year 2008.

Harry Dent may not have had a crystal ball that helped him to make uncanny predictions. What he did have though was an uncanny knack through years and years of study to be able to identify causative factors that cause ups and downs in the economy. He's been able to identify and segregate long term trends that mattered most and apply them to make forecasts years ahead. Harry applied demographic growth models to identify demographic peaks and troughs and according to his theory it is the propensity of people to consume goods and services that drives demand under-pinning economic growth. He comes up with what he calls as the generational spending wave. He explains it well in his all-time classic *ZERO HOUR* (co-authored with Andrew Pancholi, another equal adept in cycles).

Out of the vast array of cycles that influence the economy in general, he has distilled it down to four fundamental cycles that have really mattered over the last thirty or so years. Those are namely, i) The Generational Spending Wave, ii) the Geopolitical cycle, iii) The 45-year Innovation cycle and lastly iv) The Boom/ Bust Cycle.

Harry points out in his treatise Zero Hour that when even two of these cycles converge, it's distinctly noticeable and when four of them converge, it's life changing. These four have converged only twice in the last 100 or so years and that a major financial crisis and deeper downturn are almost certain when they tend to converge again.

Such was his level of confidence that Harry went on to say that if a crisis of sorts doesn't occur by 2020, he would rather quit his profession and switch his job to become a limo driver.

The Boom and the bust cycle - SENSEX (or NIFTY) vs GDP divorce

Now reverting to our discussion on bubbles, I reproduce below Harry Dent's key principles of what makes a bubble as stated in his work *ZERO HOUR*:

1. Bubbles begin when stocks or any financial asset start growing faster than linear trends. More often they start at the bottom of last major correction or crash.

2. Bubbles build exponentially for several years.

3. The greater the bubble, the greater the bust.

4. Bubbles burst twice as fast they build and more so with stocks than with commodities or real estate.

5. Bubbles tend to go back to where they started or the origin more often than not.

The bull run eventually becomes a bubble at some point in time when the stock market tends to divorce from real economic growth and starts getting ahead of itself exponentially. This presumably happens because stock markets reflect the collective enthusiasm and confidence of the masses in a fast-growing economy and vice-versa the collective lack of confidence and gloom in a bear market. The collective behaviour of investors emulates a herd mindset and investors jostling for a pie in the cake, not wanting to be missed out from a fast growing bull market.

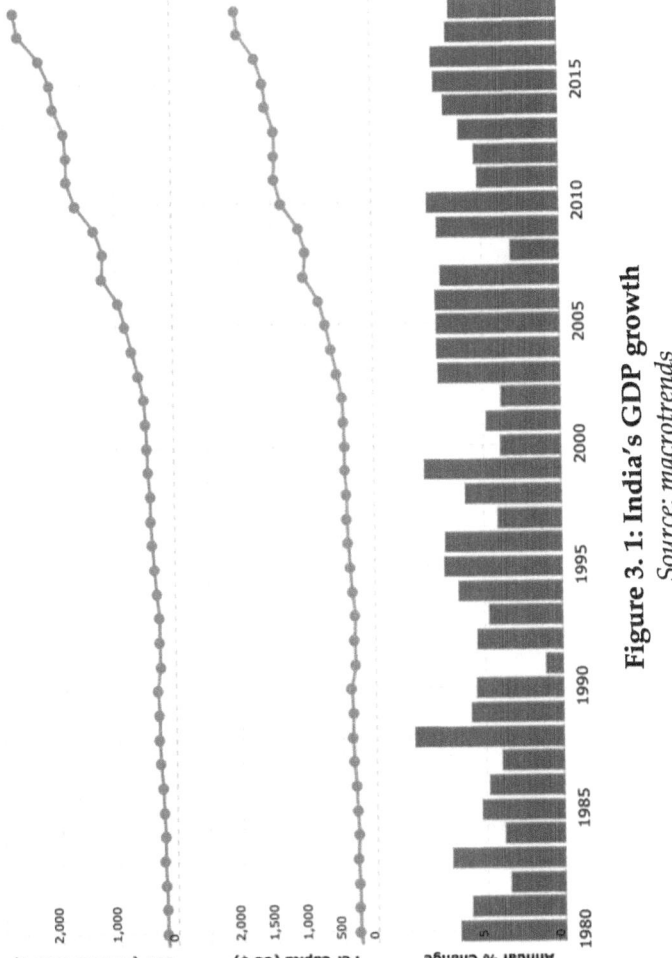

Figure 3. 1: India's GDP growth
Source: macrotrends

Refer to the Figure 3.1. In the year 2008, the GDP of Indian economy was $1.2 trillion. By 2018 it had grown over twice that size to $2.726 trillion just over twice. The future growth was expected to be faster and exponential. If you see the graph, the growth starts accelerating since the year 2008 and gains momentum a few years later again. This goes well with the rise of NIFTY and the stock market in general, which started the steepest and longest bull run in history exactly around that time.

The stock markets picked up cue and it grew at a much faster pace than the real economic growth. In 2008, BSE SENSEX - the basket of top 50 stocks comprising leaders across various industries - was 9647. By the end of 2019, the index had grown many times over to 41253 unlike the real GDP growth.

As Figure 3.2 shows, at some point in time the markets stopped growing linearly and rather started growing exponentially and that's when the bubble territory develops. The stock market was going north insanely when the economic growth rate was not necessarily growing consistently with the past and consistent with the potential and that's what we call as bubble territory.

On an average over the years NIFTY had grown at a compounded annual rate of 14%. That is what it means a stock bubble. When the market doesn't grow linearly anymore but starts growing at an exponential rate, it invariably results in a bubble and bubbles invariably explode at some point in time.

The stock market initially starts with a linear growth rate and somewhere down the line future expectations starts playing a key role as optimism and expectations about future builds up and the markets starts discounting the future growth expectations and factors it in current price. At a much later stage when the bull market is already healthy and fast paced, more and more investors figure that they may be missing out on an opportunity and start jumping in driving even more exponential growth and overheating the market in the process. That is when the bubble becomes ripe to burst and all it is looking for is a flimsy needle. If it were not a virus, it would have been still triggered by some other factor. In my opinion, the cause is irrelevant. The cause cannot be predicted in advance but we can clearly see there is a bubble and it's a matter of time before it pops up.

I have shown below the long term price chart of SENSEX to identify the bubble territory. It is important to understand the distinction here that because there is a bubble building up it doesn't mean it is devoid of economic growth nor I am claiming that that the entire thing is a farce. Let's step back and look at the pace of economic growth in India since 1980. I have also reproduced the stock market growth over the same period.

The Bubble intensity

The graph in Figure 3.2 helps to explain the bubble duration and its intensity. It would appear that the bubble phase in stock prices started somewhat in 2009 and in a more intense and serious pace in the years 2013-14. See how a linear rise eventually gave way to an exponential rise. The bubble intensity is measured as no of times gain as divided by its duration in years during the bubble phase.

I have reproduced in Figure 3.3 a snapshot of bubble intensity of various other stock bubbles from Harry Dent's *Zero Hour* for better comparison. The most relevant in my opinion is the 2009 bubble in S& P 500 as that represents a classic bubble. That one had an intensity of 0.48 as compared to the NIFTY (or SENSEX) above at 0.36. As an emerging economy with small market capitalization (compared to global peers) that just kick-started two decades ago and with much real expansion yet to take place in the decades to come, there will be potentially more bubbles to come in Indian stock market, in the long run, and those will be much bigger and make this one shrink in comparison.

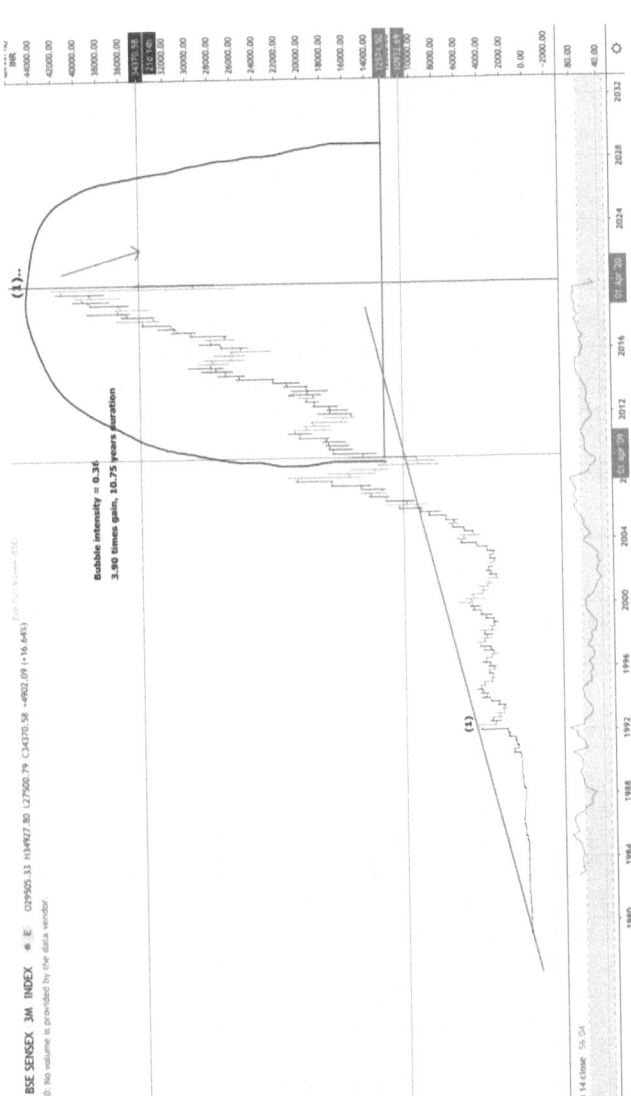

Bubble intensity = 0.36
3.90 times gain, 10.75 years duration

Figure 3.2: BSE SENSEX index quarterly chart since inception Source: tradingview

Figure 10-3: Table of Stock Bubbles Past and Present

Bubble	Start	Bubble Duration	Times Gain	Bubble Intensity	Crash Duration	Crash Severity
Nikkei, 1989	1984	5.5 Years	4.4	0.80	2.75 Years	-64%
Dow, 1929	1924	4.9 Years	3.8	0.78	2.5 Years	-89%
NASDAQ, 2000	1995	5.3 Years	6.8	1.3	2.6 Years	-78%
Shanghai, 2007	2006	1.75 Years	5.2	3.0	0.9 Years	-72%
Biotech, 2015	2011	3.75 Years	4.2	1.12	1.9 Years	-75%
S&P 500, 2017	2009	8.4 Years (Est.)	4.0	0.48	4.2 Years	-83%*

* Estimated by Model

Source: Dent Research, Bloomberg

Figure 3.3: Reproduced from Zero Hour by Harry Dent

	SENSEX	Compounded growth rate
31-Dec-19	41253	14.1%
31-Dec-08	9647	

Figure 3.4

The above table displays the NIFTY as of 31-Dec-19 and the same index as of the last bottom in Dec'08 after the financial crisis hit and when markets hit the last major bottom.

The Sensex actually hit a peak of 42273 in the ensuing weeks in early 2020 prior to Mar'20, but I have assumed the year end value for our comparison. As explained earlier, SENSEX index represents the collective value of the top stocks, which are respective industry leaders. We are talking about a compounded growth rate of 14.1% since Dec'08 year after year for SENSEX to get to where it got to in Jan'20.

The GDP measure or any productivity measure for that matter, did not experience such compounded growth rates even remotely near this rate. Now, if one may invest in an index at 14% compounded rate and earn such attractive returns with little risk, it is an investment anyone will die for.

A peek into the future

	SENSEX post-crash)	Compounded growth rate
31-Mar-20	29468	10.7%
31-Dec-08	9647	

Figure 3.5

I have plugged in the SENSEX value *post-crash* in the above table and let's see what that looks like. The compounded growth rate of NIFTY over the years post-crash is also high at 10.7%, which is way more earthly than the pre-crash 14% but still way higher than the pace of economic growth.

This reveals an interesting picture. I have assumed SENSEX at its Mar'20 lowest. Post-correction, SENSEX index, the compounded growth rate is 10.7%, which is still a very high return and many millionaires in the world will go head over heels. Any fund manager who is able to generate such consistent returns on a compounded basis will be a celebrity in his own right even after the crash.

Now, this is one of the reasons I believe the market correction is not over yet. Should the markets correct even further in the coming months and the year 2021, we would quite possibly have a more realistic SENSEX (and NIFTY) compounded growth rate and that will form an attractive bottom for building the next generation of wealth through buying stocks and building an enviable portfolio in the long run.

In my assessment, that is what the elliott wave model would seem to suggest (to be introduced in a later chapter). In fact, if Elliott wave patterns is anything to go by, the stock market bottom is *yet to come at the time of writing this book* and the next wave of correction will take the market down even deeper. The reason why I say so is that the bounce-back in stock prices since the Mar'20 crash, appears to be corrective waves and the fall in prices in Feb and Mar'20 consisted of five waves. That would suggest that the correction is not complete yet and that a next leg of correction will eventually occur sometime down the line.

Well before the crash in Mar'20, Robert Prechter the guy who for all practical purposes introduced Elliott Wave theory to the trading world and the living authority on Elliott Waves - presented to a wide audience in the New Orleans Investment conference in Nov 2019.

Prechter had accurately predicted that the markets were due for a major correction and were already at an unsustainable top.

According to wave principles enunciated by Bob Prechter, the bear market would have actually ended when sentiments turned to a negative extreme. At the time that when markets eventually hit the rock bottom, people will not be inclined to buy stocks despite being a very cheap bargain and people will be literally turning their back on equity investments.

We will have to keep a watch. Only time will prove...!!

CHAPTER FOUR

CHART PATTERNS DON'T LIE

The price action is the only thing that matters....it speaks its own language if only we understood

CHART PATTERNS DON'T LIE...

Stock prices are examined and analysed by technical traders from out of what we call as price charts. It doesn't matter whether the underlying is a stock, stock index, commodity or a currency pair. In essence, price action analysis speaks a common language regardless of the underlying instrument.

A price chart captures the i) opening price, ii) highest, iii) lowest price and *most* importantly iv) the closing price for the period. Let's say that we are looking at hourly price charts. That means each bar on the hourly price chart (or each candle in place of a bar, depending on whether you use bar charts or candlestick charts) indicates the opening and closing price aside from the highs and lows made during that period of one hour.

There was a point in time when one had to draw charts manually using end of day price as printed in the next morning newspapers. We live in a very different world now thanks to technology and advanced charting software. One is able to pull out price charts of any frequency (as long as an instrument is traded heavily) including 15-minutes, hourly, 2-hourly, daily and weekly charts and that happens interactively at real time. Today's charting platforms and software provide a wide range of analysis and indicators without a user even appreciating the calculation that goes within those indicators, which are laborious when done manually.

Technical Analysis & Price patterns

It has been scientifically demonstrated through research that price patterns as revealed in price charts foretell the future trends. In other words, future price action is not random and disjointed, but it can be deciphered broadly based on historical price patterns.

Trends are visible when you train your eyes to read long term patterns. Those interested in detecting price trends should observe price patterns in the daily chart as well as the weekly charts to understand how price is trending and especially, when one wishes to know where the markets are heading. The charts reveal in advance medium to long term price trends and key price reversals.

When you look at price charts - be it price charts of stocks, major indexes, Gold, Silver, Crude Oil or other commodities, or Forex pairs like USD EUR or USD JPY just to give a few examples - one thing is true. There's nothing new in these charts to a trained eye. What I mean is that one gets to see patterns that have occurred in the past and repeating themselves. It doesn't matter whether it is a new age Google, Amazon, Apple or Uber price chart or old age IBM, Microsoft, General Motors, Reliance or Johnson & Johnson. The price patterns do repeat like they did in the past and often tend to precede certain price paths and actions that arise subsequently.

The following are some of the well known price patterns (not an exhaustive list):

i)   Double Top

ii)   Double bottom

iii) Head & Shoulders

iv) Inverted head & shoulders

v)   Cup & handle

vi) Ascending wedge/triangle

vii) descending wedge/triangle

viii) channels (channels are not necessarily patterns but often serve the same purpose as patterns)

Technically analysis is basically understanding the language of reading price charts in order that one may anticipate or make an educated assessment as to what direction the market may move and therefore to decide whether to take a position in the market in respective instrument (stock, commodity, currency pair, index, bitcoin and whatever else.)

Many of you readers must have heard before that history repeats itself. I have heard some intellectuals assert that history does not repeat but it rhymes. However you like to put it, one observable phenomenon is that historical patterns tend to repeat themselves in similar forms and there's nothing really new in a certain sense.

Approaches to trading

A price chart can only move in so many ways, logically speaking. A stock in action is either trending upward or downward. Nearly all traders make significant profits only when the price is trending. When prices are not trending, they are said to be moving *within a range* or moving *sideways*.

There are different approaches to trading but the end objective is nearly always the same, namely, to go with the trend and make the best out of it. Some traders seek to identify the turning points when a trend is about to change and seek to ride the new trend early by catching the top (reversal from uptrend to downtrend) or catching the bottom (reversal from downtrend to uptrend).

More conservative traders don't seek to identify tops and bottoms as there is always risk of false alarms resulting in a whipsaw and having to take losses aside from having to follow the market closely. The conservative ones seek to confirm that there is a definite trend by allowing it to run and then seek to embark on it only when an uptrend or downtrend is confirmed. These traders tend to believe, perhaps rightly so, that you cannot always be part of the entire ride through a trend from beginning till the end. In other words, they are content riding a part of the trend (often the strongest or steepest part of the trend) and then jump off the train.

Whatever be the approach, knowing and identifying a trend is an essential part of the game. When markets go sideways, it's frustrating but that's also the time one has to remember to wait for the next trend to occur. When you know enough to spot a pattern, you have crossed possibly more than half the bridge in terms of knowing in advance which direction the markets may be heading.

More often than not, historical price patterns have been found to be reliable guide in predicting high probability moves in future and that provides a basis for taking an informed position. An investor or trader should always conservatively assume that his or her expectation of next price movement could go wrong. This implies that one should be prepared to accept losses for one cannot always know the future with 100% certainty. Based on analysis and by establishing threshold limits, one would set up stop losses, so as not to get whipsawed if the market moves contrary to expected direction.

The objective is not to be 100% accurate and to completely avoid losses, which is an impossible task unless you have direct access to God. The objective is to minimize losses and keep playing so that profitable opportunities make enough profit to pay for the losses and still leave substantial gains to make the entire exercise worthwhile. I'll also be honest here. Not everyone has cracked the code, but there are people around us who have been able to crack the code and consistently earn profits to make a living out of it.

A wise trader is one who analyses relentlessly and looking constantly for emerging patterns and price action. You don't have to be correct and accurate 100% of the time. In fact, a successful investor doesn't even have to be correct 50% of the times. But, that's something beyond the scope of this book and not the immediate purpose of writing this book.

Illustrations

I'll provide two real life illustrations of two listed scripts in NSE. Both these scripts took a beating in the Mar'2020 crash. A technical analyst may not have been able to predict the onslaught of the virus and the black swan event that triggered a market collapse, but he would likely have recognised the warning signs to exit these stocks, when those stocks made a new high. In fact, key NIFTY stocks like Axis Bank and Kotak Bank had shown signs of exhaustion well ahead of the market crash, which we will see later in this book.

In Illustration A, the author had articulated in advance on Jan 9'20 that the stock will hit a cap @ INR 1440 at which level it would likely collapse.

Actually, a month later the stock had exactly hit that level and took a nose-dive.

This is technical analysis and more of a chart pattern analysis and got little to do with what company A or company B is doing. A technical analyst looks at the chart, the price information and what the patterns foretell. Seriously speaking, it's irrelevant as to whether the company is listed in India, UK or US or for that matter whether it's even a stock chart or a commodity chart. So without further ado, let's look at the chart below.

Illustration A

The following is an extract from an actual analytical report alerting in advance of a price decline in ICICI Lombard stock in Jan'20 due to a preceding triangular pattern formation in the weeks between Jul'19 and Oct'19.

The above price chart was counting last stages of its first wave price cycle and will soon exhaust its bull run in ensuing weeks. Once it reaches its peak price level (which is within 6% higher from its current price levels), it is expected to commence a major decline in the weeks and months to come. It is going to be several weeks or months before eventually commencing its next higher run.

The stock price will likely move up in a spurt in coming weeks and will touch a likely high in the price range of 1440-1475. This will most likely happen in the immediate days and next couple weeks. In a less probable scenario, if the triangle gets protracted, it could take a little longer to get there.

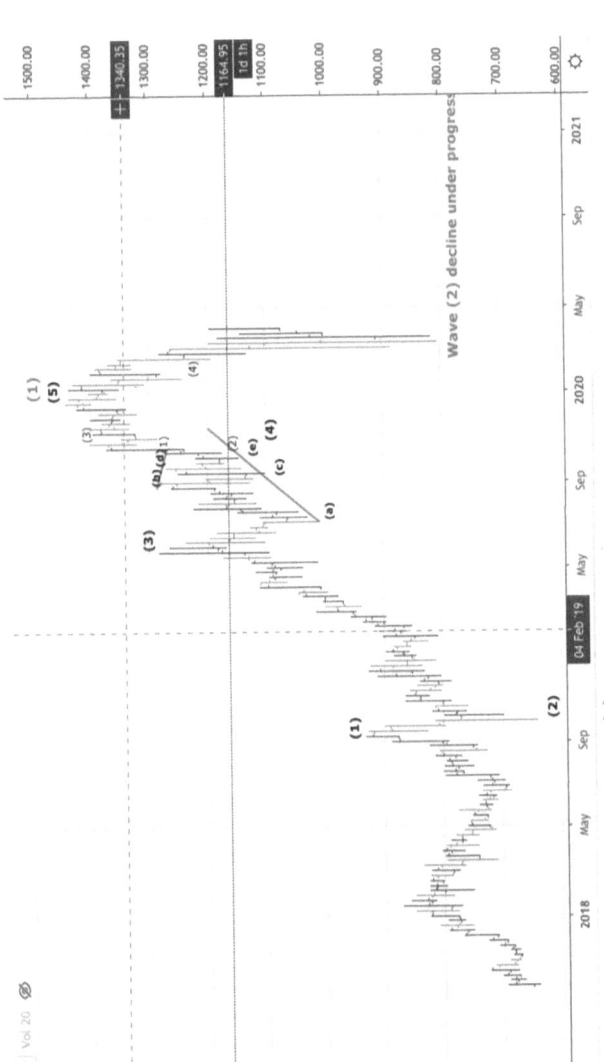

Figure 4.1: Weekly price chart of ICICI Lombard Insurance
courtesy: Trading View

ICICI Lombard continues to remain a favourable long term stock for investors with a long term horizon and who are not worried about medium term swings in the price.

The above comments were made in Jan'20 and the stock had since declined from mid-Jan at the price levels forecast earlier. The stock had since gone on a tailspin from mid-Jan at exactly the price levels forecast earlier @ INR 1440. Now, that's technical analysis working well and producing results.

The above analysis was made on the strength of a certain triangular pattern that formed on the price charts and additionally based on identifying the so-called Elliott wave patterns in the price history. A triangle pattern often indicates one last leg of price push in the same direction and then followed by a steep reversal. I just used that approach here.

Illustration B

The daily chart of HDFC Life touched a high of INR 646 in Oct'19 followed by yet another high at the same level in Jan'20 thus forming a double top pattern. It was a clear indication that the stock had reached a major top and it will encounter strong resistance at least in the medium term. The uptrend was possibly exhausted and the stock was exhibiting overbought conditions.

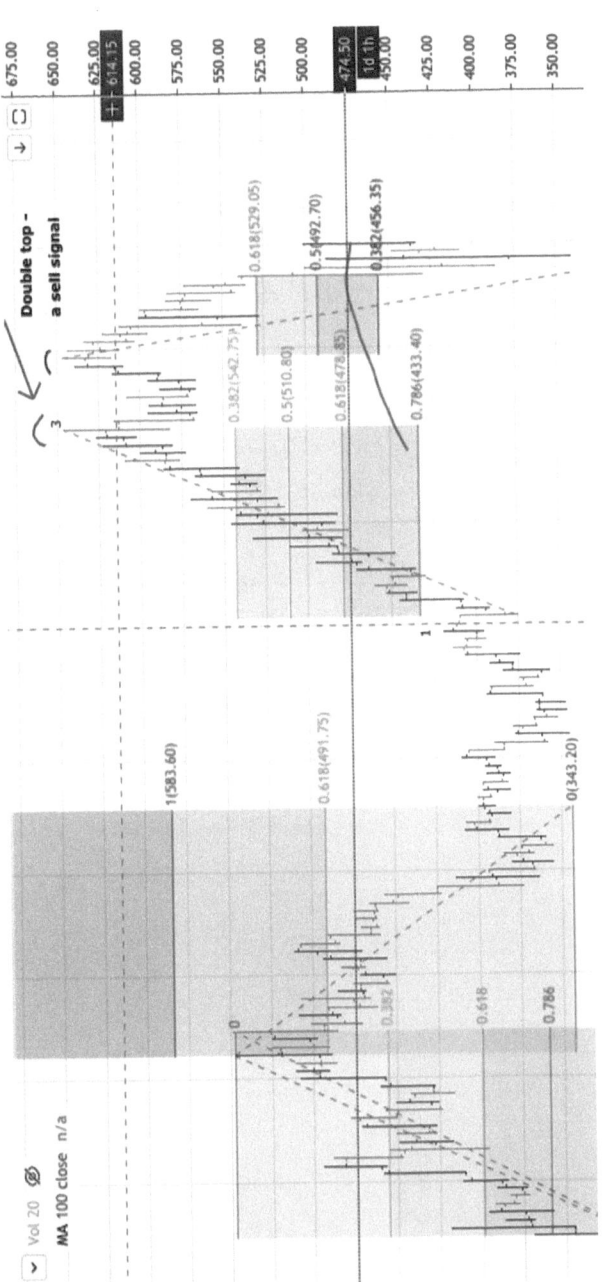

Figure 4.2: Weekly price chart of HDFC Life Insurance
courtesy: Trading View

Summary from the illustrations:

An investor could have sold after the double top was formed and booked profits in the case of HDFC Life. In the case of ICICI Lombard the triangular pattern formation was a warning of an upcoming new high to be followed by a steep decline.

In both the cases, it would have been a good strategy to book profits and protect cash-flows. Once the stock prices corrected substantially, one would re-invest in the above stocks - ICICI Lombard and HDFC Life - as both represent a new-age economy and a nascent industry that has unlimited potential in a large country. One would imagine that both were phenomenal stocks in an industry in the early stages of a very long period of growth.

PART II
A BUBBLE READY
TO BUST

CHAPTER FIVE

DIVERGENCE AMONG THE KEY INDICES

The signs of the bubble were written on the wall and visible to anyone willing *to see !!!*

— *Anonymous*

DIVERGENCE IN NIFTY 50 VERSUS OTHER INDICES

In the world that we live in and move about day to day, we are inundated with data. There's too much noise around and little focus on what matters most. We have started taking pride in being overwhelmed that we don't realize that we do not focus enough on things that matter most.

In the months preceding the Mar'2020 crash, there were ample signals that bullishness and optimism had reached unacceptable levels and a bubble was building up seriously that it could no longer be sustained. Bear in mind that this is not an academic discussion or a research dissertation.

Long term charts like monthly and weekly charts are excellent means to analyze how the market is trending and where the market may be heading, however those are not to be used for placing trades or for taking positions, which will require evaluating much shorter time intervals like a daily chart or a 2-hourly chart.

The First Signs of Exhaustion

NIFTY JR (or NIFTY NEXT 50) is the basket of 50 stocks ranking below the set of NIFTY 50 stocks, which happens to be the much watched index and basically comprise the next 50 stocks that immediately follow NIFTY in terms of market capitalisation. Those are potentially companies whose market cap is not as big as NIFTY 50 companies, but which have the potential to grow and may replace NIFTY 50 stocks over time and therefore consists of eligible candidates for an eventual promotion. In fact, in recent months, couple stocks were promoted from NIFTY JR to NIFTY 50, while couple stocks in NIFTY 50 were relegated back to either NIFTY JR or were dropped altogether from index. Some of the well known members of NIFTY NEXT 50 are DMART, HDFC LIFE and ICICI Lombard.

The chart in Figure 5.1 is a long term trend chart where each single bar indicates a month. You'll notice two thick lines on the chart for comparison, one is NIFTY Junior (also known as NIFTY NEXT 50) and the other is NIFTY 500.

Look at the right top side of the chart referred above. NIFTY JR hit its peak as early as in Dec'17. This was followed by another attempt and subsequent re-testing of its peak in Apr'18 and again in Aug'18. This is known as a *triple top pattern* and that's *a very strong bearish sign*.

NIFTY JR was facing a tight resistance and was unable to penetrate the peak it formed in Dec'17 after repeated attempts to get close to that level. NIFTY JR didn't sustain that level any longer and it eventually gave way and had since been on a steady decline after Aug'18.

In my mind, it was the ***first decisive sign*** that the nine year bull market had possibly exhausted, that growth had possibly slowed down and it was only a matter of time before the markets eventually reversed.

The entire market crashed way later in Mar'20, but NIFTY JUNIOR index clearly warned us that the economy is hitting tailwinds way back in Dec'17 and reiterated the same message again through Aug'18. In those intermediate months through 2019, there was enough news doing rounds about shrinking growth rate, rising unemployment and a complete absence of major new investments from Indian companies and near absence of large Foreign Direct investments (FDI).

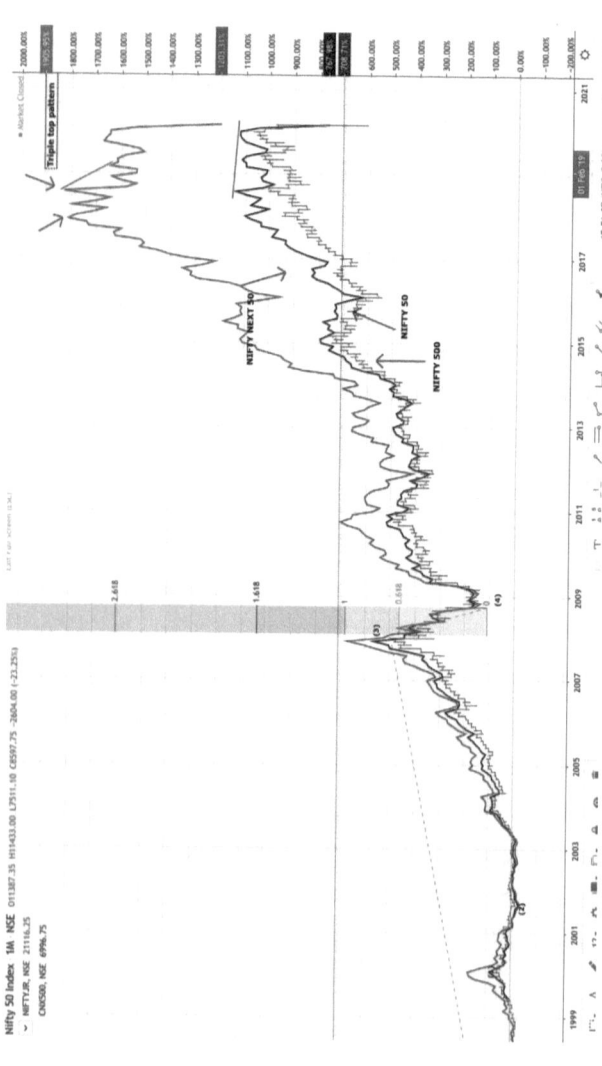

Figure 5.1: Long term monthly chart of major Indian stock indices – NIFTY, NIFTY JR & NIFTY 500

Courtesy: Trading view

Additional Signs of Exhaustion

Let's take a look at NIFTY 500, a broader basket of 500 Indian stocks and possibly the best indicator of the broader economy than select leader stocks like NIFTY 50.

The NIFTY 500 almost followed a path similar to NIFTY JR. Interestingly enough, (unlike NIFTY JR that hit a peak in Dec'17) NIFTY 500 hit a peak only later in Aug'18 and then weakly followed it up again in May'19 and Jan'20. The May'19 and Jan'20 attempts were weak in that it could not reach the same level as it did in Aug'18. It was an additional confirmation in clear terms that markets were unwilling to go any further and seemed to have reached an exhaustion. Around the same time, there were reports that economy had indeed slowed down and key parameters like GDP growth rate and job growth were starting to look bleak.

NIFTY 50 - The Rebel..!!

On the contrary, look at NIFTY 50, our crown jewel index. It was continuing to make new highs post Aug'18. In fact, between Oct'18 and Jan'20 when NIFTY 500 and NIFTY JR stock indices nose-dived, *NIFTY alone went higher up by almost 27%*. What a contradiction, or should we say the Mother of all contradictions. This is what we call a divergence or non-confirmation. In Jan'20 NIFTY made one last high while other key indices were on a decline and that was to be the last peak before the crash two months later.

Essentially, The rise in NIFTY 50 was not confirmed by other major indices. *When one key index alone rises higher, while the other key indices don't rise in tandem, then such non-confirmation indicates that something is not right and that's a bearish confirmation.*

One of the key reasons was that certain high weighted stocks in NIFTY 50 were in huge demand and those stocks prices selectively were going higher, while a majority of other stocks were not heading anywhere and many of them were already sliding down. This is also referred to in technical terms as a lack of breadth in the market and a skewed rise in stocks. I have highlighted this period with the sleeping or rising blue arrow in the chart.

The blue chip mutual funds and PMS portfolio were chasing blue chip stocks simply because they had produced cosistent and enviable returns over the past nine or so years. The easy money overseas in the form of Foreign Institutional Investors was also chasing select blue chip stocks resulting in a hefty appreciation in stock prices of those heavyweight NIFTY stocks.

The most surprising thing was that PMS and other blue chip investors assumed that somehow the blue chip stocks would continue to go up despite those stocks being terribly overvalued and the lack of breadth in the market. We would look at this more in the next chapter.

THIS IS EXACTLY THE BUBBLE TERRITORY IN STOCK MARKETS. When stock prices rise without attending rationality and economic growth and stock prices are only driven by exuberance and optimism this is what is known as bubble territory. This phenomenon went on for months before the bubble eventually exploded. We will see more of this in a subsequent chapter.

In hindsight, there is a key lesson or two for us to learn from this. I believe that NIFTY JR reflected the state of Indian economy faithfully and more accurately unlike NIFTY, which reacted with a significant time lag and crashed harder than other indices within a short span of few weeks. The institutional investors, PMS and high networth individuals, who were loaded with money were all after select NIFTY stocks and hardly anyone stopped by to read what the NIFTY JR and NIFTY 500 was pointing to all the time. The media likes to report on NIFTY 50 and SENSEX and other indices hardly ever make news.

A Sudden Crash?

Did I hear anyone say the market crashed suddenly? The market crashed no doubt, but was it sudden? The markets always crash suddenly, which is not going to change anytime in future. The question to be asked is not why markets crashed suddenly. The question to be asked is whether the markets crashed with advance alert or without any alert whatsoever. I think the answer is clear to that question.

How many news channels or news headlines report NIFTY JR and NIFTY 500? None, unless you care to visit a broker web-site or financial web-site or the NSE web-site. It pays to ignore the headlines. Stop listening to pundits and start sifting through your information. It may or may not make you rich, but it may save you huge losses and headaches right in time.

I wonder at times, how many TV channels and the pundits who appeared in them looked at the big picture and made some sense out of it. While one may not have a crystal ball to predict the future, an experienced market analyst is expected to know with some degree of confidence whether we are in an overbought territory or oversold territory, and what are the probable outcomes in order to minimize risk of loss in the portfolio.

Now, back to history...!! Back in time, there was a very famous trader known as WD Gann, who had experienced unprecedented success and had demonstrated time and again an uncanny ability to predict tops and bottoms accurately months ahead in stocks and commodities. Gann is a legend and his name evokes a sort of reverence among many of his followers even today. I remember Gann stating in one of his books that bull markets usually don't last longer than seven years in most cases. As a rare occurrence we had seen a bull run beyond nine years. Post the Lehman crisis in 2008, the next bull market had started in 2009-10 and the markets had already gone way too far in those nine years until the end of 2019.

CHAPTER SIX

IRRATIONAL EXUBERANCE CHASING STOCKS

Don't ever worry about losing an opportunity in the markets. They call it the fear of missing out. The markets never die and there are always new opportunities

– Author

HEFTY AND IRRATIONAL PREMIUM FOR THE LEADER STOCKS

Expensive stocks

There's a reason why leader stocks comprising NIFTY 50 commanded a hefty premium way more than others. Each one of those were first grade stocks, no doubts about that. But then how much premium one should be willing to pay to own a slice of action in the most valuable company. How much a premium was good enough?

Broadly speaking, financial analysts will tell you that a fair share price is determined by the earnings of a company and the so-called P/E ratio (price to earnings). Well, that sounds too simplistic and straight-forward, isn't it? Now, that's as far as mathematical or rational basis goes.

Actually, the market is not just pricing a stock for what it is worth today, but it tends to value a stock, basis what its future growth holds. Generally speaking, the market discounts future expectations of the stock, its management capability and vision, its pace of innovation and the opportunities and challenges in the industry, of which, it's a part. Now, this is where an element of subjectivity comes in. Stocks are freely traded and therefore the demand and supply factors will influence the stock prices too.

The rise of stocks from 2010 lows through 2019 was phenomenal. The bull run marks a healthy phase for the economy as it accompanies solid economic growth resulting in growth of the business and bottom-line, speaking generally. As we have already seen in preceding chapters, there comes a certain later phase in the bull market when demand exceeds supply leading to a situation, possibly caused by a high liquidity environment (or could be caused by whatever other reasons) when cheap money chases select stocks. This is when stock valuation crosses acceptable levels and reaches bubble levels.

Rising Stocks in a Downward Spiralling Economy and a Hefty Valuation of Leaders

A renowned economist and a recently awarded Nobel prize winner made a comment while visiting a leading management institute in India, wondering how on earth stock markets were cheering when economic growth was sluggish and no major economic reforms were coming forth. Reliance Industries share prices rose by a whopping 62% during this period, since mid-2018 until the end of 2019. In the same period, ICICI Bank rose by 100% and HDFC Bank stock prices rose by 41%.

There is little doubt that these represented some of the best run companies and institutions in India and should be part of any high net worth stock portfolio. That said, the rise in the stock prices represented the late stage Wave 5 (*Elliott wave parlance*) stock exuberance and optimism not substantiated by underlying economic growth and long term economic environment.

Can you believe that the market cap of HDFC Bank burst through an incremental $21 billion in the preceding year alone, and *more than any other bank in the world*?? The price to book ratio of most banks including the leaders in the developed world is at best around 2.0 and many players will have less than that ratio. A notable exception was the HDFC Bank, which had a price to book ratio of about 4.3..!! I had mentioned at that time (towards late 2019) that this valuation was simply unsustainable and what happened in the first quarter of 2020 proved that I was not wrong at all.

A few heavyweight stocks on the NIFTY index carried such disproportionate weight that just continued demand for those heavy-weight stocks gave a false sense of complacence that all is well with the markets especially given that most of the media headlines revolve around NIFTY 50 and SENSEX 30 and not other indices. As long as Foreign institutional Investors, Mutual Funds and PMS kept buying top five stocks, the indices were guaranteed to rise.

The increase in wealth levels of existing high net-worth individuals as well as rise of new wealthy population gives rise to more investments chasing stocks. The exploding middle class population in India, which is able to channel more surplus investment directly in shares and / or mutual funds also results in increase in demand for certain stocks. The other major contributing factor was the abundant and excess liquidity created in the Western world, which found its way through FPI/ FII resulting in skyrocketing stock prices.

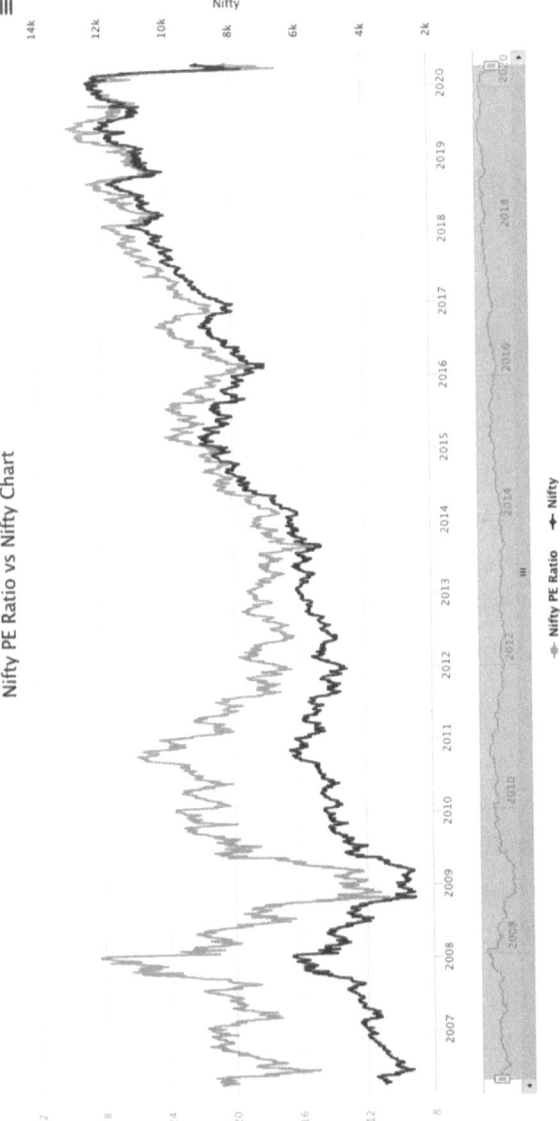

Figure 6.1: Courtesy: Equityfriend.com

Every bubble has to burst, that's universal law. The governments and central banks in the world don't have the power to stop it as much as they may seek to or claim to be able to.

Hefty PE ratios gave advanced warning signs

The above chart indeed speaks a thousand words The PE ratio indicates the price multiple the market is willing to pay for a given earnings report from the audited balance sheet of a listed company. The underlying data is made available by NSE, but I came across this incredible chart on equityfriend.com and the credit goes to them. This data is published by NSE but I liked this chart, which I came across on the website equityfriend.com.

The PE ratio of Indian stocks broadly moves within the band of 16 and 24. While minor corrections and swings occur from time to time, these swings don't indicate anything extraordinary. Any strong cyclical upswing or downside correction typically takes the curve outside the normal band.

Notice how the NIFTY PE ratio had gone up steeply all the way to 28.25 in Jan'08 prior to the correction brought about by the financial crisis.

A bubble at its peak takes the curve as far ahead as 28 as can be seen from the above.

In Apr'19, NIFTY PE ratio had touched a peak of 29.42 and again in Jun'19 it had touched an all-time high of 29.90. NIFTY nosedived steeply by 65% when the financial crisis hit the markets in the year 2008 and NIFTY PE nosedived in a matter of a few months to as low as all-time low of 12. When the markets are going through steep correction, the normal healthy band doesn't hold anymore and the NIFTY PE ratio resets itself.

I'll bet NIFTY PE ratios will never reach that peak in many years to come and when and if it does, it would be time for another major correction. I would expect that this time around in 2020 and 2021, the PE ratios will likely go as far down as the 2008 low, if not worse than that setting a new all-time record.

CHAPTER SEVEN

STAMPEDE IN THE IPO MARKET

They say change is the only constant in the world... actually change is only on the surface. Nothing ever changes fundamentally... Men and the markets are always ruled by Greed and Fear and it will remain that way. Markets are simply a reflection of collective human psychology.

– Author

STAMPEDE IN THE IPO MARKET...

An ultimate measure of greed is when a highly looked forward to IPO is oversubscribed and valuation hyped up by an obscene multiple.

The IRCTC IPO

The IRCTC IPO was the most successful IPO in 2019. The 645 crore IPO was oversubscribed 111 times. Get what that means? That means the issuers received 111 times the proposed issue, but they were legally required to return nearly all that back and only retain what was the proposed issue size. Notably, the IRCTC issue came on the heels of the bust, to be more specific, just two months before the markets made the all-time peak, which levels will not be seen at least in some years to come.

Upon its listing in mid-Oct'19, the stock started at nearly double the price and within a period of barely four months reached shy of INR 2000 (equivalent $28, give or take). Granted, IRCTC was a great listing and a viable business model and even granted that it is a monopoly in its line of business. But, nothing whatsoever changed in those four months, be it their business model, the performance results or the scope of their business or whatever other business considerations that merited a stock revaluation. If anything, the real economy was shrinking and the railway infrastructure was not undergoing any path-breaking major upgrade to warrant a change in valuation. It did not even remotely warrant a drastic change of assumptions underlying its valuation.

Notice that while valuation (that is, how much the premium market is willing to pay to own one share in the company) is heavily hyped up, nearly everyone seems to unanimously agree and there is not a voice of dissent.

For those of you who didn't track the market then, the IRCTC stock dropped during the crash all the way down to INR 775 in Mar'20 from its peak of INR 2000.

IRCTC was a great stock to hold on any day and would be an integral part of any long term portfolio. The simple point I am making is that hype and undue optimism is not sustainable beyond a point and markets do level eventually. The optimism and irrational exuberance leads to a bubble and when it gives way, it drops in a straight line. As the saying goes stocks rise in steps and drop down in an elevator.

The SBI Cards

The SBI Cards IPO was another IPO launched just weeks before the markets commenced a steep decline. The IPO was valued at around INR 750, which in my opinion was a hyped up valuation. In any business deal, both sides have to gain or else it's not a fair deal. It is normally acceptable that an IPO is valued in a manner that the issuer gets a fair premium (when it's an existing profitable business with significant growth potential). But the valuation should leave something on the table for the buyer to benefit from potential appreciation. If the buyer is already paying an exorbitant premium that's what I call a poor risk-reward ratio, skewed heavily in favor of the issuer.

There is little room for the buyer to benefit by way of capital appreciation and gains, unless he is prepared to wait for years together and by the way there is no assurance that it would indeed appreciate over the long term given many business uncertainties.

The investor is willing to pay a certain premium and wait but what is the reward for taking that risk and whether that reward is commensurate with the risk he or she undertakes. Unfortunately, most people don't think to stop by and ask the right questions and it is the herd mindset that drives market prices. (This is exactly the reason Elliott wave model works too well especially when emotions rule the market).

The fact that SBI Cards IPO was overvalued (even when bear market had just started and markets had started declining) was clear evidence of hyped up investor sentiments and optimism in its late stages. *Optimism and bullish sentiments at extremes are ripe signals for a bear market and* not *an indication of a bull market.*

Closing

The age-old demand and supply theory that you studied in the school helps to assimilate the development to an extent. Small and large investors alike are always looking for a quick way to double or triple their money and IPOs are the fastest way to get there (providing you were lucky enough to receive allotment). I am pretty sure that Paytm will regret having missed the peak of bull market for an IPO, when it could have commanded and gotten away with hyped up and perhaps absurd premiums. If it decides to go to market anytime in the next three or four years they will not even get a faint semblance of the hype that SBI Cards and IRCTC got. It is good for investors though. Now this is what you call a buyer's market.

CHAPTER EIGHT

TOO FAR....
AND FOR TOO LONG...

PRICES WENT HIGHER TOO FAR AND FOR TOO LONG....

Introduction to Elliott Wave Theory

R N Elliott was the name of a guy in the early twentieth century who intensely observed and studied stock prices and indices in the United States for months and years at a stretch and as a result of his persistence and sheer ingenuity brilliantly hypothesised what has since come to known as a wave model now known by his name by his own name. Elliott's brilliance was that he somehow observed that price patterns seemingly moved in so-called five wave and three wave cycles.

In a very brief summary, Elliott had proposed that a major trend always consisted of five impulse waves whereas corrections occurred in three corrective waves in the opposite direction of the trend. The impulse waves are usually numbered as Waves 1,2,3,4 and 5 whereas corrective waves are labelled as Waves A, B and C. Within the impulse waves, waves 1,3 and 5 were the ones in the direction of the main trend, whereas waves 2 and 4 were retracement waves (of waves 1 and 3 respectively) in the opposite direction. The impulse waves that mattered most were waves 3 and waves 5 and considered to be of utmost importance for a trader or investor.

An important observation is that the elliott waves were *fractals*, meaning the so-called waves occurred one within other in all time-frames regardless of whether it was in minutes, hours, days or weeks. For example, you will observe a 5-wave progress followed by a 3-wave correction in a 2-hr time frame and similarly in daily and weekly time frames.

Characteristics of Elliott Waves

Wave 1 starts very skeptically with few participants and there is little enthusiasm. It is then followed by a Wave 2 skepticism as buyers are skeptical and don't believe that a trend may have started, so they tend to book their profits earlier due to skepticism.

After completing wave 2, wave 3 begins and starts a new note of optimism and gradually investors starts piling in. Wave 3 builds up further and goes on making steep price advancements. In a bull market, wave 3 happens in all its glory and awe with market rise duly supported by rise in GDP growth rate and increase in business profitability and earnings.

Wave 4 marks the end of Wave 3 optimism often bringing a somewhat shallow sideways correction. Wave 5 marks the last leg in the main trend. Very often, Wave 5 does not have the same broader participation and market depth as in Wave 3, but it simply seems to replicate the optimism created in Wave 3 and stretches it far. The end of Wave 5 is marked by unmatched optimism bordering on irrational exuberance while reason and logic seems to have taken the exits. The market tops in Wave 5 is eventually followed by a significant correction in three waves A-B-C.

Elliott wave theory is now being expounded by Robert Prechter, who in my opinion, seems to know markets like the back of his hand. Robert Prechter made a presentation in a well attended investment conference in New Orleans in Nov'19 and had predicted unequivocally that stock markets had peaked and were due for a major slide down.

Wave 5 in Indian markets

In the run up to Mar'20 crash, a lot of stocks showed extended waves in Wave 5, which are marked by signals of exhaustion from a long bull run accompanied by somewhat diminishing performance results. Let us look at live examples of some leading stocks.

Illustration 1 (Maruti Suzuki)

Let's look at Maruti Suzuki, the leading automobile manufacturer and a NIFTY stock. Maruti sells the most cars in India and has arguably grown along with Indian economy through the nineties and early decades of the present century. When the economy grows, disposable income grows and one of the first things one buys is a car.

Unfortunately, it was cyclical like everything else and after long years of hectic growth, automobile sales had slowed down eventually. The diminishing sales reached a point that it grabbed so much public attention that even the Finance Minister was providing explanation as to possible reasons why car sales had declined. It was attributed to varying reasons all of which are contributing reasons including rise of rental cabs like UBER and OLA as well as drop in consumption to drop in income levels.

Maruti share price had grown from INR 400 level in the year 2004 to reach a peak just shy of INR 10,000 in Dec'17. I have marked what I believed to be wave 1, wave 3 and wave 5 terminal points. Take a look at the price chart and you will know that prices had gone way too far and for too long without a significant correction. Now, bear in mind that corrections are healthy just like falling sick is required for the body to eliminate the toxins

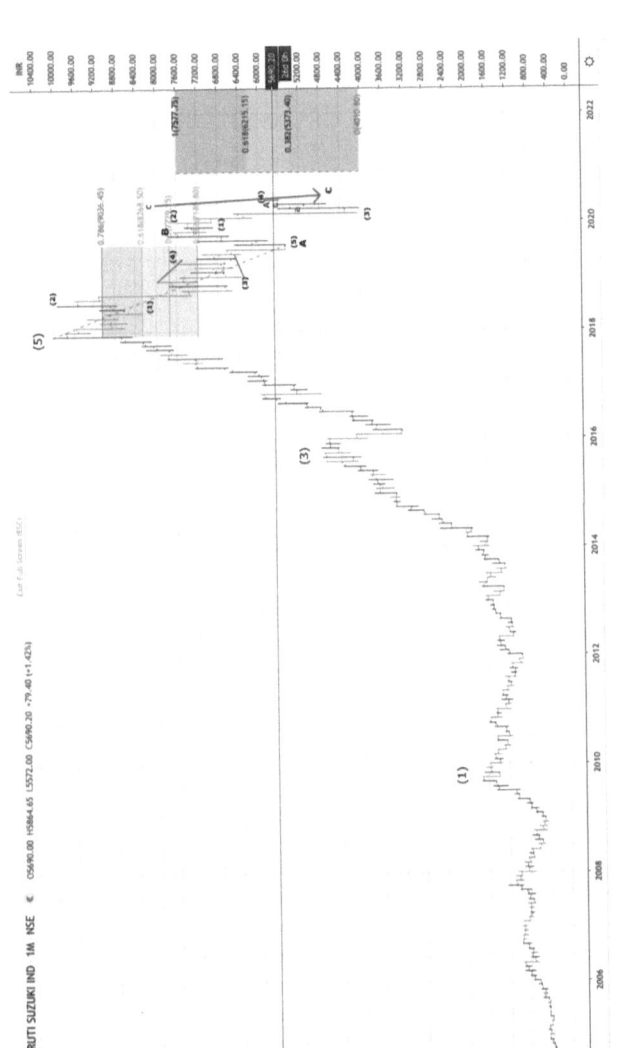

Figure 8.1: Stock price of Maruti (Monthly long term chart)
Courtesy: Trading view

and repair itself. We learn to eat the right food and the right quantity when we fall sick and also are reminded of the importance of exercising and being more health conscious once we recover. Post correction, stocks fare even better provided the company is not doing anything fundamentally wrong and the business model is keeping with the times.

The corrections are playing out exactly according to the Elliott wave model.

The steep correction in Wave A ensured that the price fell to INR 5400 level in mid-19 and there was a Wave B retracement higher up. The prices have since commenced decline in Wave C and should go down below NR 4,000 before commencing next bull wave up.

Once Maruti completes the major correction consisting of A-B-C through 2021, it will embark on an unprecedented major bullish wave up, which will make the previous rise to INR 10,000 look less significant.

Illustration 2 (TCS)

Tata Consultancy Services, popularly known as TCS, is India's answer to leadership in technology services and a stellar example of what India has contributed to in the modern world. TCS is known the world over and requires no introduction anywhere in the world.

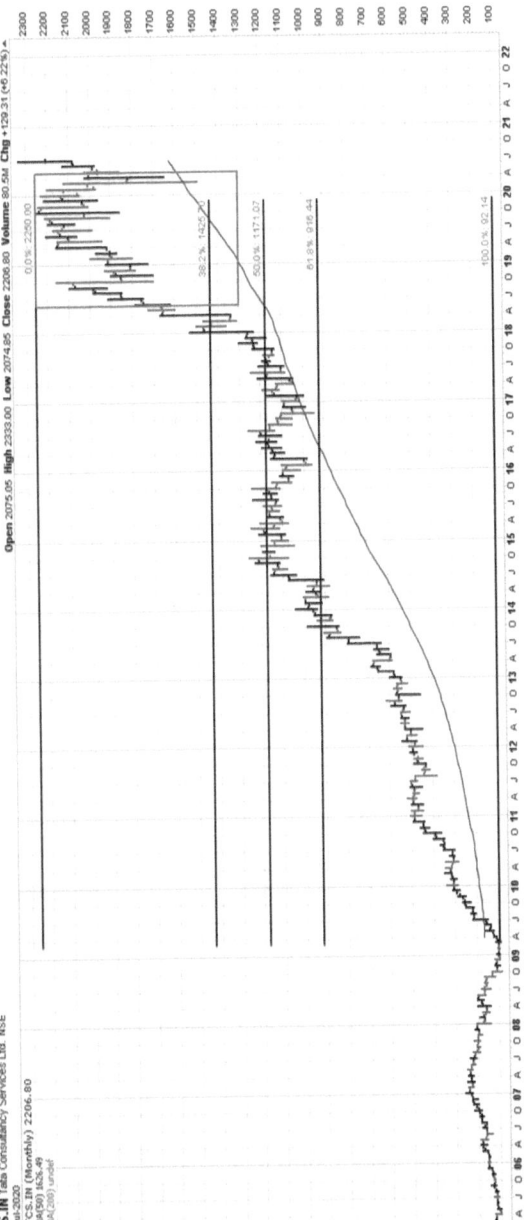

Figure 8.2: Tata Consultancy Services in place of Maruti.
Source: Stockcharts.com

TCS rose from a rock-bottom back in 2005 to a price of as high as close to INR 2300 at its peak in Sep'19. Isn't it a phenomenal rise? TCS hit some sort of a roadblock and was stuck in a range bound correction between 2018 and the Mar'20 crash. The portion is marked in rectangle in the diagram 8.2. TCS is now rising back again to an all time high and will possibly make a Wave 5 high in the coming months before resuming next wave down.

My own reading is that TCS may head down due to cyclical factors post Nov'20. and may resume a next major phase of bull run in later part of 2021.

Illustration 3 (Kotak Bank)

Kotak Bank is among the leading private banks and has shown phenomenal growth over the years, a stock most investors would like to have in their portfolio. Kotak Bank monthly chart had developed a triangular pattern in Wave 4 between Aug'18 and Feb'19, marking upon its completion, onset of the final leg of Wave 5. The triangle often than not meant that one larger wave in the direction of the main trend remained and then a steep reversal would follow. The steep correction that followed since earlier in 2020 is not surprising given the economic slow down and that the stock had gone far too long in the previous years. It's a alternating cycle of growth and decay and some price decay is inevitable before resuming next phase of growth.

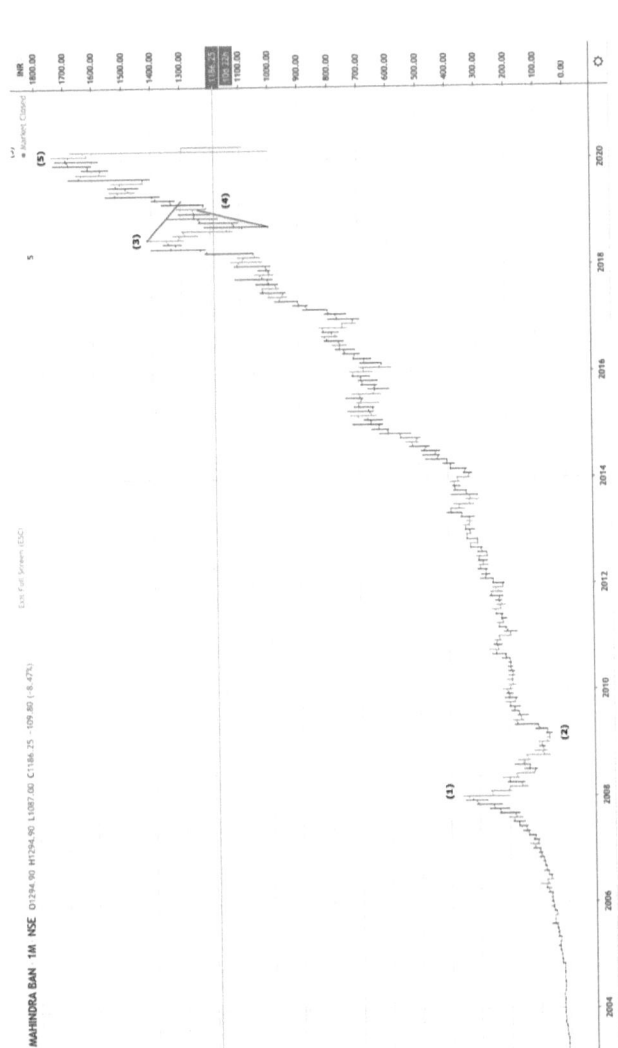

KOTAK MAHINDRA BAN 1M NSE O1294.90 H1294.90 L1087.00 C1186.25 -109.80 (-8.47%)

Figure 8.3: Monthly long term chart of Kotak Mahindra Bank
Courtesy: Trading view

Illustration 4 (Axis Bank)

There is a beautiful and classic triangular pattern that emerged in Axis Bank, another major NIFTY 50 banking stock like Kotak Bank. Yet another evidence of an impending correction.

It shouldn't be misunderstood that triangle spells doom. On the contrary, it is a conclusion based on multiple factors including a very long period of bull run without any major previous price correction coupled with a triangular pattern and certain other aspects that confirm overbought conditions.

I am certainly not claiming that one could predict the future. In fact, no one could. What we need to ask ourselves every time is which way the wind is blowing and how are odds stacked up in our favor. When the market moves against me, what is the exit strategy? Once we bring the mindset of probabilities - what is the probability that this trend will continue and what is the probability that it may not - then our whole approach becomes more realistic.

It's naive and archaic to think that one can buy stocks and sit on it forever. That is a poor investment strategy. There were enough warning signals that required us to keep our antennas up and high and told us to remain on high alert. On the contrary, a majority of investors chose to become complacent and took continuing rise and growth for granted without paying heed to warning signs.

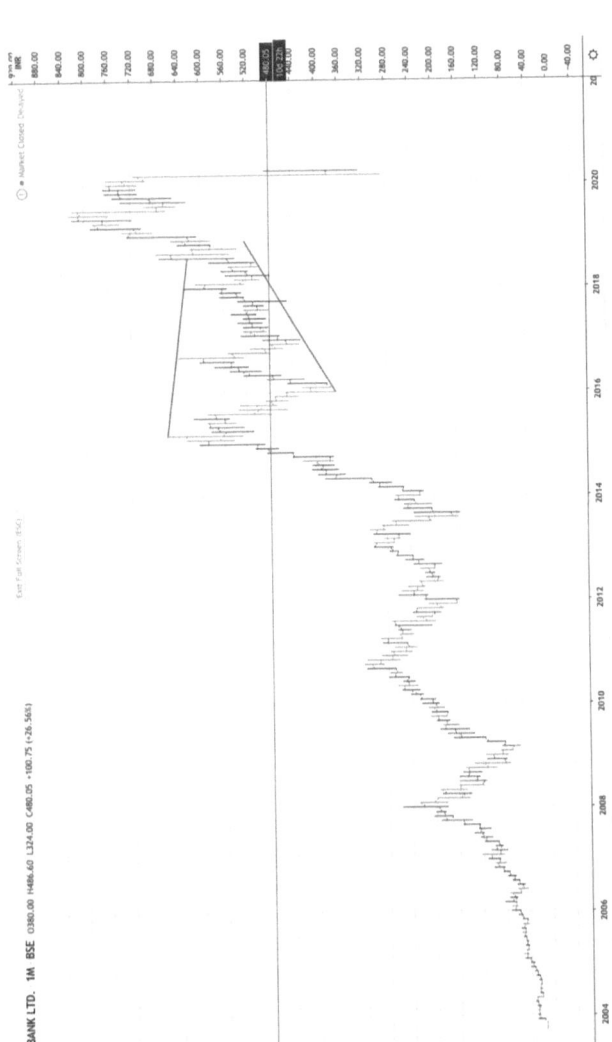

AXIS BANK LTD. 1M BSE O360.00 H486.60 L324.00 C480.05 +100.75 (+26.56%)

Figure 8.4: Axis Bank
Courtesy: Trading view

PART III

LOOKING BEYOND THE HORIZON

CHAPTER NINE

LOOKING BEYOND THE HORIZON......

WHERE ARE THE MARKETS HEADING?

It is the uncertainty of life that makes life what it is…..
Where is the charm, if everything lying ahead in future is
known and the path is certain…..??

– Anonymous

WHERE ARE THE MARKETS HEADING?

The backdrop

We are at a historic juncture and happen to be witnessing a major reversal of trends. Let's take US Dollar, which is the world currency. The dollar index has been making lower highs and lower lows over the past four decades. The dollar index has made eight or nine year high in what is a long-term declining trend over past forty five years (Figure 9.3). The international Gold prices have reached an all-time high and the appetite for Gold is ever increasing given a shaky stock market.

All leading stock indices fell steeply without exception during Mar'20 crash. Comparatively the bounceback in US indices (since the Mar'20 crash) has been strongest when you see globally. For instance, DAX (Germany) sprung back weakly as did NIFTY (India). It's not hard to see that it is possibly attributed to the fact that the Fed released a trillion dollars into the system to counter the effect of pandemic induced slowdown. Part of that money was bound to find its way into the markets and inflate the stock prices.

The bounceback of technology heavyweight NASDAQ 100 composite index has been nothing short of phenomenal. The bounceback has even gone way beyond the Mar decline and set new highs that people have even forgotten that there was a major dip earlier in the year. The pace at which the North American equity markets got back up and running made people wonder whether it is the start of a new bull market.

A record 40 million people had lost jobs and filed jobless claims since the onset of the pandemic with millions more still adding to claims and here you have the best performing quarter in the stock market in its 20-year history. *The US markets are possibly as artificially inflated as it can get and seems like a gamblers' den.*

Speaking in the Indian context, as of the time of writing these pages, NIFTY had bounced back to Fibonacci 61.8% (Refer Figure 9.1). The bounceback of Bank NIFTY has been much more subdued and weaker than the NIFTY and have retraced Fibonacci 38.2% levels.

India's GDP growth is at a historic low and spending has vastly come down due to a combination of businesses not being open as well as due to shrinking of income and spending. Those exporting services are equally challenged as overseas clients are facing a phenomenal shrinking in business and keen to cut down costs.

The impact of slowdown caused by the pandemic and possible second wave of challenges are lurking behind and pose challenges in the medium term. Most businesses that are over-leveraged and lacking efficiency are already finding it hard to sustain in tough times and stand exposed. As Warren Buffet famously said "only when the tide goes out, you will know who has been swimming naked".

Barring a few exceptions, if any, performance of companies across the board as they start releasing results will be abysmal.This is not a temporary phenomena but this lull is going to last at least for a year or two. I have seen so-called experts justifying the rally but in my humble opinion any attempt to explain the rally is simply pointless.

Stock Markets listen to no rhyme and reason as would be apparent from the recovery above. Businesses have closed and most are losing revenues. You don't have to take anyone's word for it, but results will speak for themselves in the days to come.

The one thing that is clear amidst all this is that what we are presently witnessing in NIFTY and BANKNIFTY are largely bear market rallies and it is not resumption of a fresh bull rally. I do not rule out further upside in Bank NIFTY as well as NIFTY, but **the wave** *structure and the long sideward drift confirms that the bear market is the governing trend and that it's only a matter of time when markets resume the main downward trend.*

The NIFTY BANK index had peaked to its all-time high @32000 levels in Dec'19 and had since crashed by 50% to 16000 levels. The NIFTY BANK index has since bounced back to 22500-23000 levels, now hovering around the Fibonacci 38.2 percent levels. That is clearly not a bull market rally and it represents a Wave B bounceback after a steep Wave A decline in Mar'20. I am not ruling out further bounce back in NIFTY BANK, but that doesn't change the future outlook, in my opinion. Once Wave B ends (after further bounce up in Wave B in next few months), it will be followed by another steep Wave C, which will take the markets down.

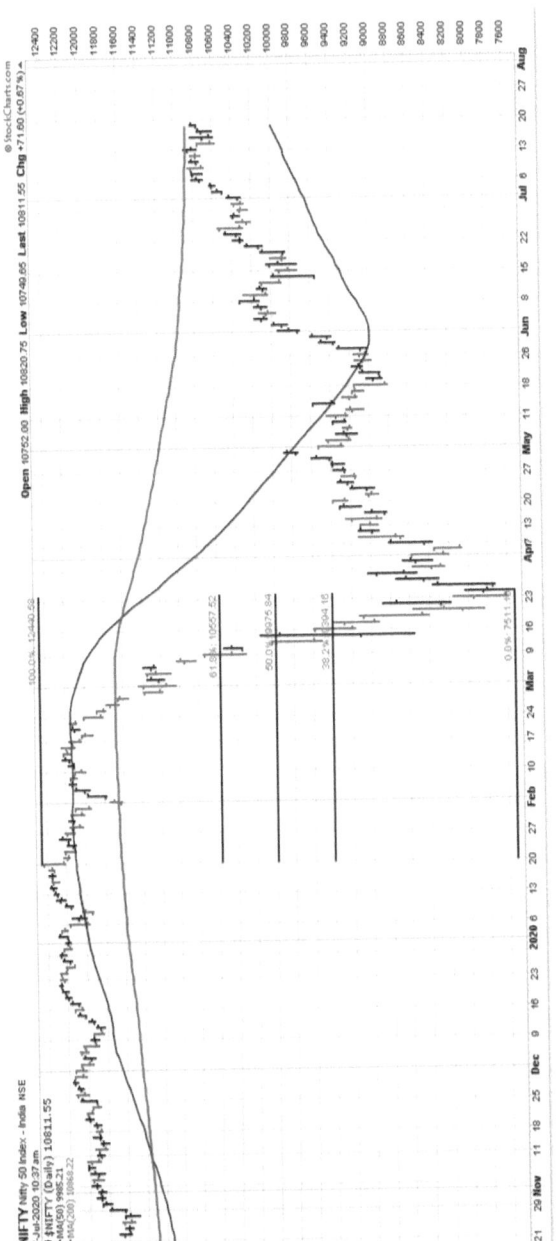

Fig 9.1 NIFTY daily chart as of week ended 17-Jul'20
Courtesy: Stockcharts.com

Gold and Dollar Index

We seem to be passing through a crucial juncture in the year 2020 and that cannot be overstated. Imagine we had the steepest market fall and stock prices didn't look this vulnerable in the past. Gold prices are peaking and even the dollar index is hovering over a peek not to speak about what happened with oil prices earlier this year.

Gold prices have reached a 8-year high and not far from the all-time high. (Refer 9.2). In the medium term, Gold seems to be heading high unhindered but, in the long run Gold will likely face stiff resistance at the all-time high levels reached in the last decade. It will form at that level what technical analysts like to call as a double top, a bearish sign. However, there is a way to go before it gets bearish. The long term Gold/ Silver ratio had been on a very steep ascent and just started reversing to a certain extent. This essentially means that Gold price expressed on the denominator of Silver prices has gone way too high and may reverse. That would mean that Silver prices having reached lows will start shooting up and potentially Gold prices may not sustain at this high level over the longer term. It is notable that the stock prices of Gold miners (companies in the business of mining gold) have been rising even faster than the pace at which gold prices have been shooting up.

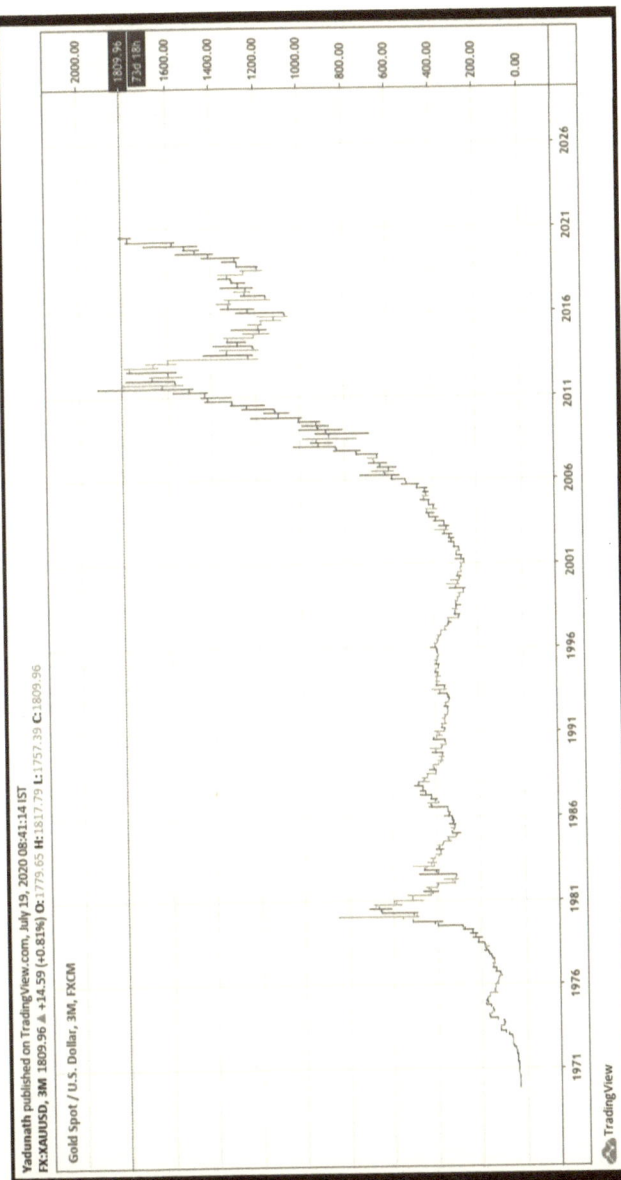

Fig 9.2 Quarterly Gold Prices over the years as expressed in dollars
Source: Trading View

As far as the US dollar is concerned, it is at a very interesting juncture and potentially may seem like a reversal point. If you see the attached dollar index chart, certain trends are obvious.

The dollar index is nothing but the strength of US dollars expressed as an index computed as a collective weight of other leading currencies. As you will agree, a currency doesn't mean much (outside of its home country) unless expressed as a factor of another currency. For example, one unit Euro doesn't mean much unless you express it as its equivalence to one US dollars or one British Pound or one Yen and so on. The dollar index is the index computed from a weighted summation of its parity in other leading currencies. A stronger dollar index would therefore mean that the US dollar is becoming dearer in other major currencies and vice-versa a weaker dollar index means it's becoming relatively more affordable in other major currencies.

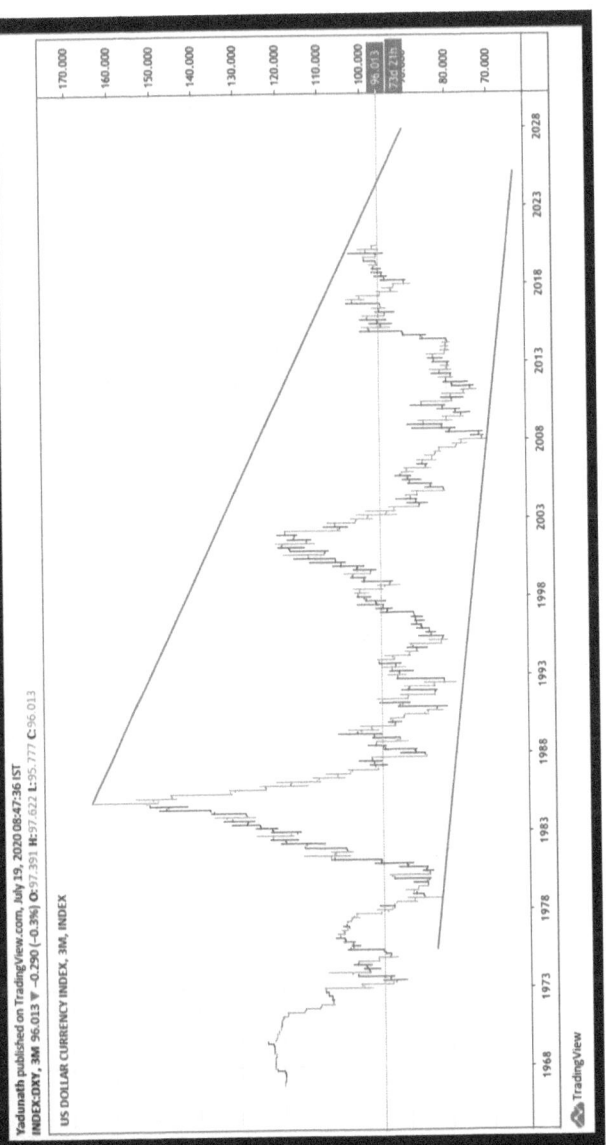

Fig 9.3 A long term trend of US Dollar index

Generally speaking, the US dollar seems to be on the decline as the attached index will show. As we span to the right side of the chart (Figure 9.3), it would seem like the US dollar is falling into an even narrower range and falling into a compression zone in the years to come. It would eventually escape its way out of the compressed triangle but that will likely take years from now.

Another interesting observation is that the US dollar index appears to go up or down in any one direction for almost 8-9 years before reversing its trend. It has moved up steadily over the recent years and seems to be hitting a roof now. Unless the dollar index pierces through the roof, which in my opinion is less probable outcome, chances are bright that dollar surge gets arrested at the present levels and it will reverse course. For all we know, it has already started reversing its course and we are just seeing the beginning of the reversal.

Indian stocks outlook

Long term Outlook

Unless you are writing a computer algorithm or preparing for an exam consisting of multiple choice questions, most of you will agree that life is not simply one of binary choices in many situations. Somebody once said that it often appears like there are no lies, it's only different layers of truth depending on one's perspective and what dimension one is looking at.

Viewed in the very long run - I mean by this over the ensuing decades - India is very likely poised for sturdy term economic growth and the topmost country with the highest growth potential. The reasons in favor of long periods of growth for the Indian economy include its potential for urbanizing for years at a stretch arising from the fact that it is among the least urbanized among large countries compared with its peers. China is the only other most populous country, which is far more urbanized than India. Demographics favor India more than any other country in the world and is heavily skewed in favor of India. In most major economies in the world, the workforce retiring is greater than those joining the workforce or will soon have that situation whereas given the youth demographics, such a situation will not arise in India at least not in

143

the immediate decades to come. India will continue to have a burgeoning youth population fueling consumer growth and whose average earnings is expected to rise for a long period to come. Of course, an underlying big assumption is that the political class doesn't completely mess up and stays clear of creating hurdles along the way - even if not facilitating economic growth.

Now, *does that mean the stock prices are going to zoom out and should we be rushing to start building up our portfolio?* No way - at least humbly in my opinion. Don't take my word or anyone else's word for it, for no one knows the future for certain. Take it with a pinch of salt - if not armful of salt - and tread with caution. In order to succeed in the market, you don't need predictive power into the future. All you need is awareness and action while time will guide you as long as you are keeping aware and have your strategy well-defined.

Medium term outlook

In the medium run, the path is rough and challenges abound. As someone said recently, India has never had a negative growth in forty years and that distinction could go to the present government for the first time. Already the central bank projections point to an unprecedented shrinking in the first quarter and such is its cumulative effect that the overall growth for the year could as well be negative. We shall wait and see.

We, in India, have not seen many bear markets unlike North America, which has a stock market history of over a hundred years and there is no dearth of bear markets in their history. Interestingly, the ones that hit the west or, rather the bear market depressions that *originated* in the west - the Financial Crisis in the year 2008 and the Dot Com bubble in the year 2000 - impacted Indian markets as well and till date remain our best bear market reference points.

The impact of the dot com bubble in the year 2000, lasted for nearly 18 months before the markets commenced a bull run again. The impact of the financial crisis in the year 2008 - the last bear market to hit us - lasted for close to nine months. In any case, the fall in Mar'20 is much more severe and steeper than what hit us in the years 2000 and 2008 respectively. It's only natural to expect that the bear market would last for some time and we cannot wish it away after six weeks of price decline in Feb-Mar'20.

What the NIFTY may hold?

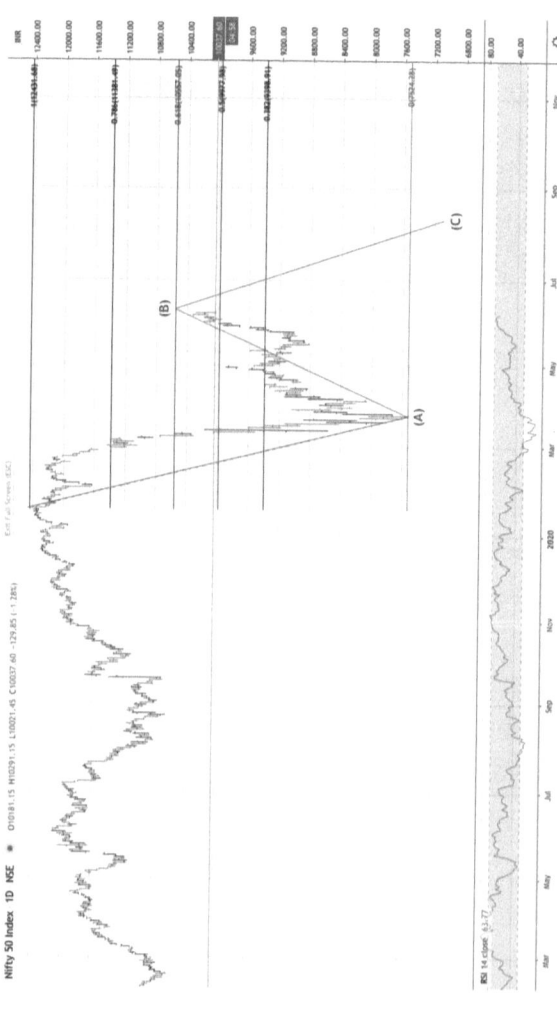

Fig 9.4 A snapshot of NIFTY index taken in early Jun'20

Courtesy: Trading view

Figure 9.4 is a snapshot of NIFTY (daily chart, where each bar indicates a day) taken on 9-Jun'20.

A quick look at the stock chart will tell you many things. NIFTY had reached an all-time high of 12430 on 20-Jan-20. Nearly 40% of NIFTY as of 20-Jan-20 was simply wiped out in a matter of about eight weeks time and most of that happened in even fewer weeks, though eight weeks is the time it took from one extreme to another. *It must be noted that 80% of the above decline happened within just three weeks time through Mar'20.*

Now, back to our graph of NIFTY downfall since the onset of 2020, notice that I have labeled as Wave A the downfall of NIFTY to 7500 levels. The subsequent rise, which I have said earlier is on a weak note, is no mark of a bull run. There is always some section of the population that believes that stocks are a cheap buy after a 40% slide and think it's a good time to buy.

While it's one thing to be bold and optimistic, all the progress can only be achieved in future. Nobody can wish away current reality. Wherever you wish to get to, the first step has to be taken from where you are, so we have to first acknowledge the present situation, whatever the future target or ambitions maybe.

Economy has contracted over the last quarter and recovery will be slow. There is no real reason to have a stunning bull market now and should you see one, beware it is deceptive and unsustainable over time.

Elliott Wave model (dealt with elsewhere in this book) states that all decline takes place in three waves. *The key decline between Feb and Mar'20 was a Wave A decline* and the bounce back or retracement since last week of March 20 *is a Wave B bounceback,* which is still under way.

Please refer to the 9.4 for a better understanding of the wave labels. Based on the Elliott Wave principle, the minimum one should expect is a three wave correction (A-B-C), so once wave B exhausts itself, another steep wave of decline (Wave C) shall commence. The bounceback in Wave B will go on somewhat until Oct or Nov of this year.

The markets will eventually run out of steam towards last quarter and then will commence another round of decline. At the minimum, it will bring the market down to below Mar'20 levels, if not much below those levels. This implies that the best time to buy is not here yet and one should exercise more patience before starting to build a long term portfolio again.

It's better to remain flexible and not start labeling waves when waves are yet unfolding. It often happens that as the markets unfold, one has to review the labels and modify as necessary and as called for. That said, the next direction is pretty clear. Whether these are still sub-waves of a much larger correction ahead or whether there is only one more major wave down left, whichever it is, *the next occurrence will be Wave C down*.

For those of you interested to track the markets alongside, it would be my endeavor to share ongoing details on a web-site or else follow up this book with another updated edition. Whichever way that is, we will stay tuned for the action as it occurs.

One round of decline will possibly occur towards last quarter of 2020 and another round of more severe correction will likely occur in later part of 2021. The financial year 2021-22 will likely be a very challenging year for the Indian stock markets. The markets may not be ripe for investing for the most part. The cycles appear to suggest that while markets may witness a rally (post US elections), the rest of the year will be busy undoing that rally. Once the market indeed hits a bottom in 2021-22, the Indian stock markets will present a lifetime opportunity towards the start of 2022 and that in my opinion will be the foundation for what is possibly one of the best phases of a bull market we will get to witness in our lifetime.

Let the Automobile sector guide you

In my considered view, the automobile industry is by far among the most reliable indicator of economic performance. When the real economy is growing and prospering, it reflects most in the automobile industry because transportation of both people and goods tend to increase rapidly with rising economic activity. When an economy grows, it's invariably reflected in a growing consumption of automobiles. Aside from cars and SUVs, most importantly trucks have to distribute goods from factories to delivery points and key harbors like JNPT in Mumbai.

Tata Motors and Ashok Leyland will sell more and report more top-line growth. As agricultural growth picks up, Eicher will manufacture and sell more and more tractors. I can imagine very few other sectors as such reliable indicators as automobile industry is.

When an economy grows, the automobile sector is the first one to announce that to the world and vice-versa when an economy shrinks, the automobile sector is among the first affected.

Look at the picture of Maruti Suzuki down below. Maruti is the bellwether stock for the automobile sector and as pointed out the automobile sector reveals the true economic growth most often as compared to other sectors.

The Maruti stock price is arguably the best representation of what India's economic growth potential is and a representative sample of what it could accomplish. The stock grew many times over to a touching distance of INR 10,000 in Dec'17 (from a low of INR 178 in 2003..!!) and see what happened afterwards..!! The stock drifted apart and had fallen to a 3-year low of INR 4,000 in Mar'20. It's hovering over INR 5,000 as I write this page. Is it a good buy? It certainly is, because Maruti is nowhere about to disappear in the foreseeable future. The down arrow you see in the picture was drawn by me months ago.

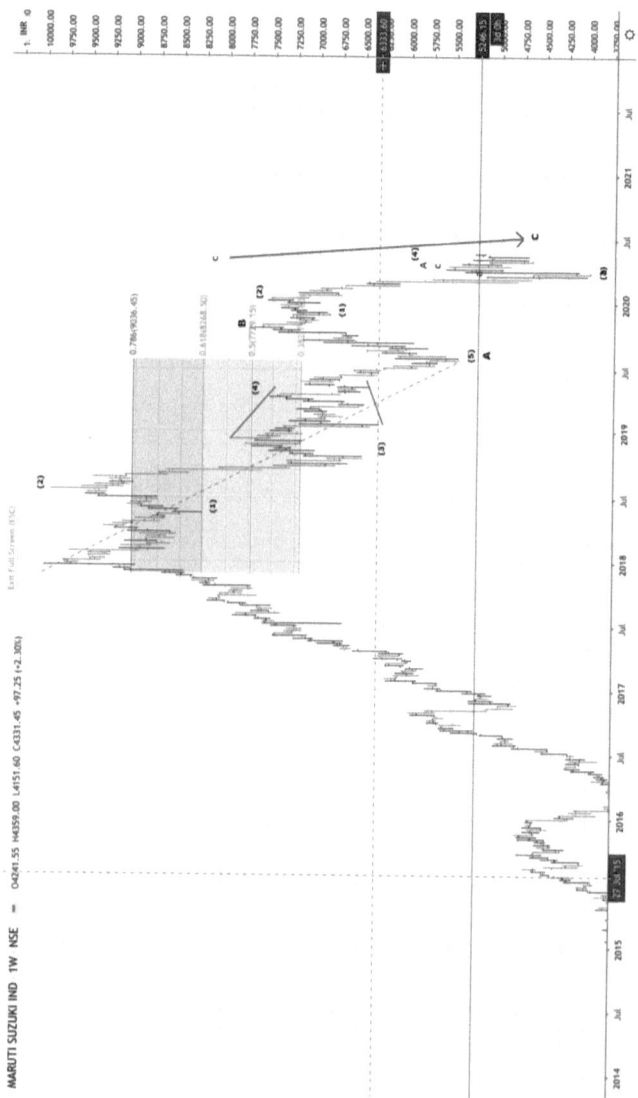

Fig 9.5

The truth is that Maruti demonstrated the slowdown of Indian economy miles ahead of most other NIFTY stocks, especially the darling stocks that most investors went after head over heels just before the crash took place between Feb and Mar'20. *In my opinion, Maruti will be among the first major stocks to announce the return of growth years and prosperous times ahead.* It would perhaps appear that the stock has still not reached a bottom though I should hasten to add that the bottom is not far from where the stock is presently. The stock is not likely to show any hurry in the year 2020, but the Maruti stock will be among the first to announce the herald of good times ahead and that will likely be some time before the end of the year 2021.

It is important to understand that as an investor you are not required to pick bottoms and tops accurately. Most professional fund managers would struggle to do so, much less ordinary investors with less time and expertise with them. You have to be only part of the ride to grow your wealth and you don't necessarily have to board that growth train from the starting point. Much like a train takes in passengers in between, there are always points where you will be able to board the stock train. You just need to watch and stay aware.

Let Maruti and the larger auto sector guide you. When Maruti hits the bottom that marks the low point of Indian economy. When Maruti starts rising, that will promise a ticket to a rising land of growth, wealth and prosperity. These words may seem like an exaggeration but the true test of any theory or prediction is time and only time will prove the merit.

Conclusion:

In conclusion, the Indian stock markets may have come to a slumber now, but it's bound to turn the corner in the ensuing year and a half or two. Once the markets have corrected fully, the next bull market will likely be even stronger and bigger than the one we have seen in preceding years. India is poised for hectic economic growth in the decades to come and that is bound to reflect in the stock market. There is no better way and better time to build wealth than riding on the top NIFTY 50 stocks and NIFTY JR stocks during a period of unstinted economic growth. Building wealth through investing in markets takes patience and attention and patience will be amply rewarded. I wish every reader a safe and happy investment journey.

Always bear in mind to play out safe in markets and follow strict risk management norms. In case of doubts as to what is the most suitable investment strategy for you, don't hesitate to approach a SEBI certified investment advisor.

Acknowledgements and Notes

1. Classic text "Elliott Wave Principle" by Frost & Prechter was used as a reference.

2. The Sale of a Lifetime by Harry S.Dent Jr. was used as a reference.

3. Zero Hour by Harry S.Dent Jr. and Andrew Pancholi was used as a reference,

4. The price charts printed in this edition were generated from third-party sites under paid subscription and the source has been attributed below the respective charts within the book. The author likes to profusely thank and acknowledge TradingView and StockCharts.

5. Certain charts and diagrams (other than stock and index price charts) were sourced through third-party web-sites and the source has been acknowledged below respective diagrams and charts. The author likes to individually thank each one of those sources for helping to drive home a point and make this book complete.

6. The wave counts presented in Chapter 8 are based on the author's own assessment of what may constitute high probability wave counts and subject to ongoing review and modifications. The author does not make any assertion that the wave counts displayed in the charts are the most accurate. The author acknowledges that alternate assignment of wave counts are possible as long as they fulfill the guidelines and rules stated in the Elliott Wave Principle.